6th Workshop on NLP for Computer Assisted Language Learning and 2nd Workshop on NLP for Research on Language Acquisition

Held at NoDaLiDa 2017

NEALT Proceedings Series Volume 30

Gothenburg, Sweden
22 May 2017

Editors:

Elena Volodina　　　　**Gintare Grigonyte**
Ildiko Pilan　　　　　 **Kristina Nilsson Bjorkenstam**
Lars Borin

ISBN: 978-1-5108-4337-0

Proceedings of the Joint

6th Workshop on NLP for Computer Assisted Language Learning
and
2nd Workshop on NLP for Research on Language Acquisition

at NoDaLiDa 2017
Gothenburg, 22nd May 2017

edited by

Elena Volodina, Ildikó Pilán, Lars Borin,
Gintarė Grigonytė and Kristina Nilsson Björkenstam

Preface

For the second year in a row we have brought the two related themes of NLP for
Computer-Assisted Language Learning and NLP for Language Acquisition together
under one umbrella. The goal of organizing these joint workshops is to provide a
meeting place for researchers working on language learning issues including both
empirical and experimental studies and *NLP-based applications*.

The **theme on Natural Language Processing (NLP) for Computer-Assisted
Language Learning (NLP4CALL)** is a meeting place for researchers working on the
integration of Natural Language Processing and Speech Technologies in CALL systems
and exploring the theoretical and methodological issues arising in this connection.

The intersection of Natural Language Processing and Speech/Dialogue Technology with
Computer-Assisted Language Learning (CALL) brings "understanding" of language to
CALL tools, thus making CALL intelligent. This fact has given the name for this area of
research – Intelligent CALL, ICALL. As the definition suggests, apart from having
excellent knowledge of Natural Language Processing and/or Speech/Dialogue
Technology, ICALL researchers need good insights into the second language acquisition
(SLA) theories and practices, as well as knowledge of second language pedagogy and
didactics. Hence, this workshop covers all ICALL-relevant research, including studies
where NLP-enriched tools are used for testing SLA and pedagogical theories, and vice
versa, where SLA theories/pedagogical practices are modeled in ICALL tools.

The **workshop on Natural Language Processing (NLP) for Research in Language
Acquisition (NLP4LA)** broadens the scope of this joint workshop to also include
theoretical, empirical, and experimental investigation of first, second and bilingual
language acquisition.

We believe that this field will benefit from collaboration between the NLP, linguistics,
psychology and cognitive science communities. The workshop is targeted at anyone
interested in the relevance of computational techniques for first, second and bilingual
language acquisition. Therefore, our aim is to bring together researchers from different
fields with a shared interest in language acquisition.

For the two tracks we invited submissions:

- that describe research directly aimed at ICALL
- that demonstrate actual or discuss the potential use of existing Speech
  Technologies, NLP tools or resources for language learning
- that describe the ongoing development of resources and tools with potential
  usage in ICALL, either directly in interactive applications, or indirectly in
  materials, application or curriculum development, e.g. collecting and annotating
  ICALL-relevant corpora; developing tools and algorithms for readability

Elena Volodina, Lars Borin, Ildikó Pilán, Gintarė Grigonytė and Kristina Nilsson Björkenstam 2017. Preface.
*Proceedings of the Joint 6th Workshop on NLP for Computer Assisted Language Learning and 2nd Workshop
on NLP for Research on Language Acquisition at NoDaLiDa 2017.* Linköping Electronic Conference Proceedings 134: i–vi.

analysis, selecting optimal corpus examples, etc.

- that discuss challenges and/or research agenda for ICALL
- that describe empirical studies on language learner data
- that describe computational models of first, second and bilingual language acquisition
- that describe empirical or experimental studies, or computational models of various aspects of language and their effect in language comprehension and acquisition
- that demonstrate actual or discuss the potential use of Speech Technologies, NLP tools or resources for investigating language acquisition
- that describe psycholinguistic and socio-linguistic investigations on first, second and bilingual language acquisition

We have encouraged paper presentations and software demonstrations describing the above-mentioned themes for the Nordic languages; and papers that focus on different age groups, cultures, and language variation.

This year we had the pleasure to welcome invited speakers from the two research areas: Torsten Zesch (University of Duisburg-Essen) and Bente Ailin Svendsen (University of Oslo).

Torsten Zesch leads the Language Technology Lab[1] at University of Duisburg-Essen, Germany. He holds a doctoral degree in Computer Science from Technische Universität Darmstadt and has worked as a substitute professor at the German Institute for International Pedagogical Research. His research interests include the processing of non-standard, error-prone language as found in social media and learner language. He also focuses on exercise generation for computer-assisted language learning and automatic assessment of free-text answers and essays.

In his talk *Automatically _____ gap-fill exercise items* he gave an overview of the work done by him and his colleagues on automatically generating and scoring gap-fill exercise items. This covered early experiments on trying to find low-ambiguity contexts, the follow-up work on generating challenging distractors, and finally the recently introduced gap-fill bundles.

Bente Ailin Svendsen is Professor of Second Language Acquisition and Scandinavian Linguistics. She initiated and co-developed MultiLing Multilingualism in Society across the Lifespan[2], a Center of Excellence funded by the Research Council of Norway (RCN), where she was the Deputy Director 2013-2015. She has carried out research on multilingual socialisation, competence and use among children and adults; and on linguistic practices and identity constructions among young people in multilingual urban spaces. Her publications include the book Language, Youth and Identity in the 21st Century. Linguistic Practices across Urban Spaces (co-edited with Jacomine Nortier, Cambridge UP, 2015), Multilingual Urban Scandinavia: New Linguistic Practices (co-edited with Pia Quist, Multilingual Matters, 2010), as well as articles in the European Journal of Applied Linguistics, International Journal of Bilingualism and Nordic and Norwegian journals and books.

---

1   http://www.ltl.uni-due.de/
2   http://www.hf.uio.no/multiling/english/

In her talk *The dynamics of citizen science in exploring language diversity* she explored the dynamics of citizen science (CS) in sociolinguistics, i.e. the involvement of non-professionals in doing sociolinguistic research, coined as Citizen Sociolinguistics (Rymes and Leone 2014, Svendsen, pending for review). In 2014, Norwegian pupils in all grades were invited to become citizen scientists through a national research campaign. Data from 4500 pupils reveal a vast linguistic diversity, an eagerness to learn languages, and a widespread use of English on a daily basis. The results, however, reflect prevailing hierarchical language regimes, firstly in the selection of specific 'foreign' languages offered and the desire of pupils to learn them, and secondly in the fact that the pupils' home languages are not actively used in the classroom. In the talk, Bente argued that one of the main advantages of Citizen Sociolinguistics is its wide-reaching potential and that it represents a method suited for collecting big data sets. Secondly, it is argued, based on a media analysis of the above CS-study, that CS has a potential to increase linguistic awareness and thus stimulating linguistic stewardship. However, CS raises some challenges for sociolinguistic research, ethically, as well as ontologically and epistemologically: what do CS-data represent and what claims can be made from them? Epistemologically, with a CS methodology, we are decentralising authority on who holds legitimate knowledge about language. Citizen Sociolinguistics is about opening the dialogue between 'the academy' and the 'citizens', it stimulates public engagement and it has a potential to advance the social impact of sociolinguistics.

Rymes, Betsy and Andrea R. Leone. 2014. Citizen sociolinguistics: A new media methodology for understanding language and social life. *Working Papers in Educational Linguistics* 29(2): 25–43.

Svendsen, Bente Ailin, pending for review. The dynamics of citizen science in sociolinguistics. *Journal of Sociolinguistics*.

Svendsen, Bente Ailin, Else Ryen and Kristin Vold Lexander. 2015. *Rapport fra Forskningskampanjen 2014: Ta tempen på språket![3]* [Report on the Research Campaign 2014: Taking the temperature of language!]. Oslo: Norwegian Research Council.

Previous workshops

This workshop follows a series of workshops on NLP for CALL – and lately in combination with NLP for LA – organized by the NEALT Special Interest Group on Intelligent Computer-Assisted Language Learning (SIG-ICALL[4]). The workshop series has previously been financed by the Center for Language Technology[5] at the University of Gothenburg, and Swedish Research Council's conference grant.

Submissions to the six workshop editions have targeted a wide variety of languages, ranging from well-resourced languages (Chinese, German, English, French, Portuguese, Russian, Spanish) to less-resourced ones (Erzya, Estonian, Irish, Komi-Zyrian, Meadow Mari, Saami, Udmurt, Võro), among which several Nordic languages have been targeted: Danish, Estonian, Finnish, Icelandic, Norwegian, Saami, Swedish, and Võro.

The wide scope is also evident in the affiliations of the participating authors as shown in

---

3   https://www.miljolare.no/innsendt/oppslag/1336/5502d9f97a260/rapport_fd2014.pdf
4   http://spraakbanken.gu.se/swe/forskning/ICALL/SIG-ICALL
5   http://clt.gu.se/

Table 1:

Country	2012–2017
Australia	2
Belgium	4
Canada	3
Denmark	1
Estonia	3
Finland	6
France	3
Germany	42
Iceland	3
Ireland	2
Japan	2
Norway	10
Portugal	4
Russia	10
Slovakia	1
Spain	3
Sweden	51
Switzerland	8
UK	1
US	3

Table 1. Authors by affiliations, 2012-2017

So far, acceptance rate has varied between 50% and 77%, the average being 60% (see Table 2). The acceptance rate is rather high, however, the reviewing process has always been very strict with two-three double reviews per submission. This indicates that submissions to the workshops have always been of high quality.

Workshop year	Submitted	Accepted	Acceptance rate
2012	12	8	67%
2013	8	4	50%
2014	13	10	77%
2015	9	6	67%
2016	14	10	71.5%
2017	13	7	54%

Table 2. Submissions and acceptance rates, 2012–2017

Acknowledgements

We gratefully acknowledge the financial support from the Department of Linguistics at Stockholm University regarding the keynote speaker Bente Ailin Svendsen, and to the Department of Swedish Language at the University of Gothenburg, that provided funding for the invited speaker Torsten Zesch. We would also like to thank our Programme Committee who did a wonderful job reviewing papers:

- Lars Ahrenberg, Linköping University, Sweden
- Florencia Alam, CONICET, Argentina
- Christina Bergmann, Centre National de la Recherche Scientifique, France
- Eckhard Bick, University of Southern Denmark, Denmark
- Lars Borin, University of Gothenburg, Sweden
- António Branco, University of Lisboa, Portugal
- Jill Burstein, Educational Testing Service, USA
- Piet Desmet, KU Leuven Kulak, Belgium
- Simon Dobnik, University of Gothenburg, Sweden
- Thomas François, UCLouvain, Belgium
- Gintarė Grigonytė, Stockholm University, Sweden
- Anna Gudmundsson, Stockholm University, Sweden
- Björn Hammarberg, Stockholm University, Sweden
- Katarina Heimann Mühlenbock, DART, Sahlgrenska Universitetssjukhuset, Sweden
- Sofie Johansson, University of Gothenburg, Sweden
- Chigusa Kurumada, University of Rochester, USA
- Peter Ljunglöf, Chalmers University of Technology, Sweden
- Ellen Marklund, Stockholm University, Sweden
- Detmar Meurers, University of Tübingen, Germany
- Kristina Nilsson Björkenstam, Stockholm University, Sweden
- John K. Pate, The University at Buffalo, USA
- Martí Quixal, Univeristat Oberta de Catalunya, Spain
- Lena Renner, Stockholm University, Sweden
- Gerold Schneider, University of Konstanz, Germany
- Mathias Schulze, University of Waterloo, Canada
- Philip Shaw, Stockholm University, Sweden
- Jennifer Spenader, University of Groningen, Netherlands
- Sofia Strömbergsson, Karolinska Institutet, Sweden
- Joel Tetreault, Yahoo! Labs, USA
- Cornelia Tschichold, Swansea University, UK
- Francis Tyers, The Arctic University of Norway, Norway
- Sowmya Vajjala, Iowa State University, US
- Paul Vogt, Tilburg University, Netherlands
- Elena Volodina, University of Gothenburg, Sweden
- Torsten Zesch, University of Duisburg-Essen, Germany
- Robert Östling, Stockholm University, Sweden

We intend to continue this workshop series, which so far has been the only ICALL- and LA-relevant recurring event based in the Nordic countries. Our intention is to co-locate the workshop series with the two major LT events in Scandinavia, SLTC (the Swedish Language Technology Confrence) and Nodalida, thus making this workshop an annual event. Through this workshop, we intend to profile ICALL and LA research in Nordic countries and beyond, and to provide a dissemination venue for researchers active in this area.

Workshop website:
https://spraakbanken.gu.se/eng/icall/joint6thNLP4CALL-2ndNLP4LA2017

Workshop organizers

Elena Volodina, Ildikó Pilán, Lars Borin (University of Gothenburg)
Gintarė Grigonytė, Kristina Nilsson Björkenstam (University of Stockholm)

Contents

Learning with Learner Corpora: using the TLE for Native Language Identification

Allison Adams and Sara Stymne
Linguistics and Philology
Uppsala University
`aadams297@gmail.com,sara.stymne@lingfil.uu.se`

Abstract

This study investigates the usefulness of the Treebank of Learner English (TLE) when applied to the task of Native Language Identification (NLI). The TLE is effectively a parallel corpus of Standard/Learner English, as there are two versions; one based on original learner essays, and the other an error-corrected version. We use the corpus to explore how useful a parser trained on ungrammatical relations is compared to a parser trained on grammatical relations, when used as features for a native language classification task. While parsing results are much better when trained on grammatical relations, native language classification is slightly better using a parser trained on the original treebank containing ungrammatical relations.

1 Introduction

Native Language Identification (NLI), in which an author's first language is derived by analyzing texts written in his or her second language, is often treated as a text classification problem. NLI has proven useful in various applications, including in language-learning settings. As it is well-established that a speaker's first language informs mistakes made in a second language, a system that can identify a learner's first language is better equipped to provide learner-specific feedback and identify likely problem areas.

The Treebank of Learner English (TLE) is the first publicly available syntactic treebank for English as a Second Language (Berzak et al., 2016). One particularly interesting feature of the TLE is its incorporation of an annotation scheme for a consistent syntactic representation of grammatical errors. This annotation system has the potential to be useful to native language identification, as the ability to parse ungrammatical and atypical dependency relations could improve the informativeness of dependency-based features in such a classification task.

Assessing this potential has been accomplished by training a parser on the original treebank and using it to extract dependency relations in a learner English corpus. Those dependency relations were then used as features in a machine learning classification task. The success of this classification was then assessed by comparing the results to a classification on features extracted by a parser trained on the error-corrected version of the treebank, based on the assumption that the original version of the treebank will more accurately handle grammatical errors in learner texts. This is a novel approach in that other similar experiments have used dependency parsers trained on grammatical treebanks to extract dependency relations.

We found that using the original version of the corpus gave slightly better results on native language classification than using the error-corrected version. However, when we investigated parsing results, the original version gave much lower results on parsing both for original and error-corrected texts. This seems to suggest that there is useful information in the types of errors made by this parser.

2 Related Work

2.1 L1 Identification in L2 Texts

As mentioned in the previous section, the task of native language identification (NLI) involves determining a writer's first language (L1) by analyzing texts produced in their second language (L2). Language learner data is used to train clas-

Allison Adams and Sara Stymne 2017. Learning with learner corpora: Using the TLE for native language identification. *Proceedings of the Joint 6th Workshop on NLP for Computer Assisted Language Learning and 2nd Workshop on NLP for Research on Language Acquisition at NoDaLiDa 2017.* Linköping Electronic Conference Proceedings 134: 1–7.

sifiers, such as support vector machines (SVM), for predicting the L1 of unseen texts. One of the first studies carried out in automatic L1 detection (Koppel et al., 2005) classified L2 texts using features such as function words, part-of-speech bigrams, and spelling and grammatical errors. The features were evaluated on a corpus of learner English, and the researchers ultimately found that by combining all of the features using a SVM, they could achieve an accuracy of 80.2% on the International Corpus of Learner English (ICLE) (Granger et al., 2002). Wong and Dras (2011) extended this study to include the use of syntactic features for this task by extracting features from parse trees produced by a statistical parser. In doing this, they incorporated production rules from two parsers: the Charniak parser as well a CFG parser. Other studies such as Swanson and Charniak (2012) make use of tree substitution grammars as a source of features for NLI. Several studies, such as Tetreault et al. (2012), Brooke and Hirst (2012), and Swanson (2013) have tested a range of features including dependency features, as well as combinations of features to ascertain which feature or ensemble of features is most useful. In doing so, they demonstrated the value of dependency features in classifying the L1 of texts.

In the case of Brooke and Hirst's study (2012), when running their system on both the FCE and the ICLE, after testing the usefulness of a range of different types of features, they found dependency features to provide a muted benefit to their system, with cross-validation resulting in accuracy scores of 61.4% for the ICLE and 45.1% on the FCE. They noted, however, that other features were more useful. Tetreault et al (2012) also tested a wide range of different types of features, testing their system also on the ICLE as well as the TOEFL11 corpus. By increasing the dependency relation feature set by including several different types of back-off dependency representations (described in section 3.2), they were able to raise accuracy of classification on the ICLE corpus to 77.1%, and reported an accuracy of 70.9% on the TOEFL11 corpus. Furthermore, the authors of the study found that classification accuracy was lowest for languages in the corpus with a high concentration of high-proficiency test responses, and best for higher concentrations of medium proficiency responses.

2.2 Universal Dependencies and the Treebank of Learner English

Dependency parsing has been rapidly gaining popularity over the past decade and differs from the older traditional constituency parsing in that in a dependency tree, the words are connected to each other by directed links (Kübler et al., 2009). The main verb in a clause assumes the position of the head, and all other syntactic units are connected to the verb by their links or dependencies to the head (Kübler et al., 2009). Annotated treebanks are typically used to generate dependency parsing models. The Universal Dependencies (UD) Project is a recent effort aimed at facilitating cross-lingual parsing development through the standardization of dependency annotation schemes across languages (Nivre et al., 2016). A central aspect to the UD project is the creation of open-source treebanks in a variety of languages that can be used to facilitate cross-lingual parsing research. All of the treebanks have been annotated according to the UD annotation scheme, in order to ensure consistency in annotation across treebanks. These guidelines have been developed with the goal of maximizing parallelism between languages (Nivre et al., 2016).

The Treebank of Learner English (TLE) is a part of the UD project and is a manually annotated syntactic treebank for English as a Second Language (Berzak et al., 2016). It includes PoS tags and UD trees for 5,124 sentences from the Cambridge First Certificate in English (FCE) corpus (Yannakoudakis et al., 2011). The treebank is split randomly in to a training set of 4,124 sentences, a development set of 500 sentences and a test set of 500 sentences. Ten different language backgrounds are represented in this corpus: Chinese, French, German, Italian, Japanese, Korean, Portuguese,Spanish, Russian and Turkish. For each language background, the TLE contains 500 randomly sampled sentences from the FCE data set, in order to ensure even representation. All sentences included in the TLE were selected so that they contain grammatical errors of some kind. The creators of the treebank exploit a pre-existing error annotation scheme in the FCE, adapting it to fit UD guidelines. In this scheme, full syntactic analyses are provided for the error corrected and original versions of each sentence. This in conjunction with additional ESL annotation guidelines provide for a consistent syntactic treatment of ungrammat-

Language	Low	Medium	High
Arabic	296	605	199
Chinese	98	727	275
French	63	577	460
German	15	412	673
Hindi	29	429	642
Italian	164	623	313
Japanese	233	679	188
Korean	169	678	253
Spanish	79	563	458
Telugu	94	659	347
Turkish	90	616	394
Total	1330	6568	4202

Table 1: Score level distributions in TOEFl11

ical English.

2.3 TOEFL11 Corpus

The TOEFL11 corpus was designed specifically with the task of NLI in mind, and comprises 12,100 learner essays written as a part of the standardized English language test, TOEFL (*Test of English as a Foreign Language*) (Blanchard et al., 2013). As the name of the corpus implies, 11 language backgrounds are included in the corpus: Arabic, German, French, Hindi, Italian, Japanese, Korean, Spanish, Telugu, Turkish, and Chinese. These language backgrounds are distributed evenly across the corpus, with 1,100 essays per language, and an even sampling across responses to eight different prompts. All essays have been graded according to proficiency as *high*, *medium*, or *low*, and have not been sampled evenly across L1s. The thought behind this is that proficiency score distributions in the corpus ought to correspond to the real-life score distributions in test results, as this information may be relevant and useful to L1 classification. The distribution of score levels per language can be found in Table 1.

3 System

3.1 Parsing the corpus

For the purposes of this paper, five dependency parsers were trained using MaltParser (Nivre et al., 2007). Three parsers were trained using the TLE as a training corpus. We also trained two contrastive parsers on the English Web Treebank (EWT), a UD treebank of English containing documents from five genres: weblogs, newsgroups, emails, reviews, and Yahoo! Answers (Silveira et

	Sentences	Words
TLE	4124	78541
EWT	12544	204586
EWT 50%	6272	101101

Table 2: Size of the training corpora for the parsers.

al., 2014). The sizes of the treebanks are shown in Table 2. The EWT is substantially larger than the TLE. In order to investigate the effect of corpus size to some extent, we also used half of the EWT to train a parser.

Of the three parsers trained on TLE, the first parser was trained on the original version of the TLE (containing grammatical errors), while the second parser was trained on the corrected version of the TLE. A third parser was trained on a hybrid version of the original and corrected treebanks, the driving idea behind this being that while the corrected version of the treebank would be ill-equipped to model grammatical errors in dependency parse trees, the original version of the treebank, in which every sentence contained at least one error, would be hard-pressed to accurately model entirely grammatical sentences. To keep the size of all three treebanks consistent, the merged treebank was created by taking every other sentence from the original and corrected treebanks. In this scheme, the same sentences (save for the minor differences in the corrected sentences) are represented in all three treebanks. Because MaltParser requires texts to be part-of-speech-tagged in order to be parsed, the HunPos part-of-speech tagger (Halácsy et al., 2007), trained on the EWT was used to acquire PoS tags for each document in the TOEFL11 corpus. All three parsers were then run on each part-of-speech-tagged document using default parameter settings, resulting in three individual parsed data sets.

In order to estimate the accuracy of the parsing models, we evaluated them on three test sets from the TLE, original, corrected, and merged, created by applying the same process described earlier. The accuracy of the parsers is assessed by means of labeled and unlabeled attachment scores (LAS and UAS), the results of which can be found in Table 3. As established by Berzak et al. (2016), parsers trained on both the corrected and original versions of the TLE outperform the parser trained on a standard English treebank, with the merged

Train Set	Test Set	LAS	UAS
TLE$_{corr}$	corrected	**94.5**	**95.6**
	original	**90.1**	**92.2**
	merged	**92.5**	**94.1**
TLE$_{orig}$	corrected	85.7	88.5
	original	85.1	88.0
	merged	85.2	88.0
TLE$_{merged}$	corrected	85.0	88.1
	original	85.0	88.0
	merged	85.4	88.0
EWT	corrected	80.7	86.0
	original	80.6	86.1
	merged	80.8	86.0
EWT 50%	corrected	79.8	85.4
	original	79.3	85.0
	merged	80.0	85.5

Table 3: Parser accuracies for all three test sets.

version of the TLE following this trend as well. Interestingly, however, and contrary to assumptions made in the beginning of this paper, the parser trained on the corrected version of the treebank considerably outperformed both the original and merged versions of the treebank on all three test sets. The two parsers trained on the EWT had considerably lower scores than any parser trained on TLE. The difference in training data size between the two EWT parsers was small, in comparison.

3.2 Using dependency arcs as features

Similar to most other NLI systems, in this paper, the task of native language identification is approached as a text classification problem. In order to solve this classification problem, dependency relations were extracted from each document to be used as frequency-based features. To do this, a system similar to the one presented in (Tetreault et al., 2012) was used, with the main difference being that MaltParser, rather than the Stanford Dependency parser was used to obtain them. This system, represented below in Table 4, can be described as follows: each basic dependency relation, consisting of the dependency label, the parent node, and the child node is extracted from the sentence. To mitigate sparsity, each dependency in the document was represented in several different ways. In the first representation, the lemmas for the root and child node were used to form the dependency relation. Secondly, part-of-speech tags were considered instead of lemmas, with dependency relations consisting of the dependency la-

dep(lemma, lemma)	(lemma, lemma)
dep(PoS, lemma)	(PoS, lemma)
dep(lemma, PoS)	(lemma, PoS)
dep(PoS, PoS)	(PoS, PoS)

Table 4: Types of dependency relations used in feature set

bel, one lemma, and one PoS tag, or a dependency label and two PoS tags. Lastly, the corresponding dependency relations without labels were also incorporated into the feature set. In this work we only used parsing-based features and do not combine them with other feature sets. From the parsing output for each parsing model on the 12,100 essays in TOEFL11 corpus, we extracted on average just over 1.5 million features. Once the feature set was established, a support vector machine (SVM) was used to classify the data set. Scikit Learn's LinearSVC (Pedregosa et al., 2011), which is powered by liblinear (Fan et al., 2008), set with default parameter settings was used to carry out the classification.

3.3 Results

To evaluate the three systems, we used 10-fold cross-validation. As the classification report featured in Table 5 shows, differences between the three models trained on TLE were negligible, with the model based on the original version of the TLE slightly outperforming the other two models across all metrics, but to only a very marginal degree (a couple of tenths of a percentage point most often). The model trained on the full EWT preformed as well as the model trained on the original TLE, whereas the model trained on half EWT had the lowest core of all models. This indicates that the size of the corpora is indeed important, and that considerably more out-of-domain data is needed to have a performance on par with smaller in-domain data.

The hybrid model, which contained features extracted by a parser trained on a merged version of the original and corrected treebanks performed nearly as well as the model based on the original treebank. Contrary to our hypothesis that higher parser accuracy ought to correlate to a higher classification accuracy, despite having LAS and UAS scores nearly five points above the other TLE two models, the corrected model had the lowest classification performance of the three. The full EWT model with a much lower parsing accuracy also

Proceedings of the Joint 6th Workshop on NLP for Computer Assisted Language Learning and 2nd Workshop on NLP for Research on Language Acquisition at NoDaLiDa 2017

	Acc	P	R
Original	70.5	70.7	70.6
Corrected	70.2	70.3	70.3
Merged	70.5	70.6	70.5
EWT	70.5	70.7	70.6
EWT 50%	70.0	70.1	70.0

Table 5: Accuracy, precision, recall for native language identification with the three parser models.

Language	Original	Corrected	Merged
Arabic	**68.0**	66.1	67.0
Chinese	74.3	**74.7**	73.5
French	70.1	71.0	**71.2**
German	81.5	**82.5**	81.7
Hindi	**64.7**	64.2	64.3
Italian	75.9	**76.2**	75.8
Japanese	**71.3**	70.5	**71.3**
Korean	63.7	62.7	**64.5**
Spanish	62.2	62.7	**62.9**
Telugu	**71.5**	71.1	71.3
Turkish	**72.1**	70.7	71.6

Table 6: Accuracy scores by language for all three models

performed on par with the best TLE model. This can also be compared to the 70.9% classification accuracy obtained using dependency relations as features in the study carried out by Tetreault et al. (2012), in which a standard English treebank was used, which however used both a different parser and different dependency relations. However, it still indicates that although all three TLE models perform relatively well, under this experimental set-up, using dependency features based on those found in the TLE does not improve results compared to using larger standard treebanks. On the contrary, these results point toward a negative correlation between parser and classification accuracy. This could indicate that, to some degree, the classification may actually be aided by the differences in types of errors the parser makes when it encounters ungrammatical syntactic constructions.

A more detailed breakdown of the model accuracies by language (found in Table 6) provides a limited degree of insight into why this is the case. Most accuracies within languages across the models varied only by a few tenths of a percentage point, with the largest deviations found in Arabic (with a 1.9 percentage point difference between the original and corrected models), Turkish, (1.4 percentage point difference between original and corrected models), and German (with a 1 percentage point difference between the original and corrected models). It had been expected that the most accurate parsing model would be best equipped to classify the languages with the highest concentration of low and medium proficiency scores, and would result in a less accurate classification for the languages in the corpus with a higher number of high scoring documents. This intuition is based on the notion that the former set of languages would have a greater percentage of erroneous dependency structures that would be consistently captured by the parsing model. The results, however, show this not to be the case. For example, Arabic and Turkish, both of which had a relatively low number of high scoring responses, preferred the original model, which had a much lower parser accuracy. This is further reinforced by the German classification accuracies, which had the highest concentration of high scoring responses, and was one of the only languages for which the corrected model performed best. It is also interesting to note that with German being the most accurately classified language, this goes against the findings of Tetreault et al. (2012), that high-profiency texts are generally harder to classify, suggesting that this trend does not hold for dependency-based classification. This also supports the notion that parser errors made due to ungrammatical dependency relations may help classification.

The surprising consistency across all three models may in fact show the degree of influence that part-of-speech tags have on MaltParser's output, regardless of the parsing model used to parse the data set. This might also reflect an underlying problem in the methodology. Due to factors of both convenience, and concerns about sparsity, HunPos, the part of speech tagger used to generate the PoS tags needed to be able to parse the corpus, was trained on the EWT, a Standard English corpus. As a result, the part of speech tags used were the same across all three models, which may have resulted in a larger degree of similarity across the dependency relations than had been anticipated. Furthermore, because the tagger was trained on texts generated by largely L1 speakers, the distribution and make-up of the part of speech tags projected on to TOEFL11 corpus might not be reflective of those found in the TLE. Furthermore, in their study, Berzak et al. (2016) note that systematic differences in the EWT annotation of various parts of speech compared to the Universal Dependencies guidelines might also negatively affect performance. As Berzak et al. (2016) also found that combining the TLE with the EWT improved parsing accuracy and PoS tagging accuracy on their test set, an interesting point for future research could be applying that technique to this study, to see if results could be improved. In particular, it could be interesting to see if using this model to acquire part of speech tags has any affect on classification accuracy.

An additional possibility for future research, which lies outside of the scope of NLI, relates to the results of the parser accuracy tests described in section 3.1. The considerable improvement in parser accuracy on the uncorrected learner essays when trained on the corrected version of the treebank has intriguing implications for the automatic annotation of learner data. This should be further explored in future work, including a detailed error analysis of these results.

There are several ways in which this study could be improved with regard to NLI. In this work we did not optimize any of the models used. A further possibility is to combine our parse features with previously suggested features, such as language model features (Tetreault et al., 2012) or character n-grams (Ionescu et al., 2014). It would also be interesting to investigate if unlabeled learner data can be used to improve both the parsing results on learner texts and NLI.

4   Conclusion

This study investigated the potential of the use of the Treebank of Learner English to improve Native Language Identification. To do this, we proposed using the original version of the TLE, the corrected version, as well as a hybrid version consisting of sentences from both versions of the treebank to train three dependency parsing models using MaltParser. Each of those models was used to extract dependency relations from the TOEFL11 corpus, which were in turn used as features in a text classification task. While the classification model using features obtained using the original version of the TLE had better scores than the other two models, the differences in accuracy scores across all three models were small. It is interesting

that even though the parser trained on the original model had slightly better classification results, it also had substantially lower parsing results than the parser trained on the corrected model. We also trained a contrastive system on the much larger English Web Treebank, which had even lower accuracy on parsing learner data, but performed on par with the TLE system on native language classification, while a parser trained on 50% of this treebank did not perform well. This provides an indication that both the size and domain of the training corpus are important.

Acknowledgment

We would like to thank the three reviewers for their valuable comments, as well as Yevgeni Berzak for his help with providing the updated version of the corrected and original versions of the TLE. We would also like to thank the participants of the course Language Technology: Research and Development in Uppsala for their feedback on a first version of this paper.

References

Yevgeni Berzak, Jessica Kenney, Carolyn Spadine, Jing Xian Wang, Lucia Lam, Keiko Sophie Mori, Sebastian Garza, and Boris Katz. 2016. Universal dependencies for learner English. In *Proceedings of the 54th Annual Meeting of the Association for Computational Linguistics*, pages 737–746. Association for Computational Linguistics.

Daniel Blanchard, Joel Tetreault, Derrick Higgins, Aoife Cahill, and Martin Chodorow. 2013. TOEFL11: A corpus of non-native English. *ETS Research Report Series*, 2013(2):i–15.

Julian Brooke and Graeme Hirst. 2012. Robust, lexicalized native language identification.

Rong-En Fan, Kai-Wei Chang, Cho-Jui Hsieh, Xiang-Rui Wang, and Chih-Jen Lin. 2008. LIBLINEAR: A library for large linear classification. *Journal of machine learning research*, 9(Aug):1871–1874.

Sylviane Granger, Estelle Dagneaux, Fanny Meunier, and Magali Paquot. 2002. *International corpus of learner English*. Presses universitaires de Louvain.

Péter Halácsy, András Kornai, and Csaba Oravecz. 2007. Hunpos: an open source trigram tagger. In *Proceedings of the 45th annual meeting of the ACL on interactive poster and demonstration sessions*, pages 209–212. Association for Computational Linguistics.

Radu Tudor Ionescu, Marius Popescu, and Aoife Cahill. 2014. Can characters reveal your native language? a language-independent approach to native language identification. In *Proceedings of the 2014 Conference on Empirical Methods in Natural Language Processing (EMNLP)*, pages 1363–1373. Association for Computational Linguistics.

Moshe Koppel, Jonathan Schler, and Kfir Zigdon. 2005. Automatically determining an anonymous authors native language. In *International Conference on Intelligence and Security Informatics*, pages 209–217. Springer.

Sandra Kübler, Ryan McDonald, and Joakim Nivre. 2009. Dependency parsing. *Synthesis Lectures on Human Language Technologies*, 1(1):1–127.

Joakim Nivre, Johan Hall, Jens Nilsson, Atanas Chanev, Gülsen Eryigit, Sandra Kübler, Svetoslav Marinov, and Erwin Marsi. 2007. Maltparser: A language-independent system for data-driven dependency parsing. *Natural Language Engineering*, 13(02):95–135.

Joakim Nivre, Marie-Catherine de Marneffe, Filip Ginter, Yoav Goldberg, Jan Hajic, Christopher D Manning, Ryan McDonald, Slav Petrov, Sampo Pyysalo, Natalia Silveira, et al. 2016. Universal dependencies v1: A multilingual treebank collection. In *Proceedings of the 10th International Conference on Language Resources and Evaluation (LREC 2016)*.

F. Pedregosa, G. Varoquaux, A. Gramfort, V. Michel, B. Thirion, O. Grisel, M. Blondel, P. Prettenhofer, R. Weiss, V. Dubourg, J. Vanderplas, A. Passos, D. Cournapeau, M. Brucher, M. Perrot, and E. Duchesnay. 2011. Scikit-learn: Machine learning in Python. *Journal of Machine Learning Research*, 12:2825–2830.

Natalia Silveira, Timothy Dozat, Marie-Catherine de Marneffe, Samuel Bowman, Miriam Connor, John Bauer, and Christopher D. Manning. 2014. A gold standard dependency corpus for English. In *Proceedings of the Ninth International Conference on Language Resources and Evaluation (LREC-2014)*.

Ben Swanson and Eugene Charniak. 2012. Native language detection with tree substitution grammars. In *Proceedings of the 50th Annual Meeting of the Association for Computational Linguistics: Short Papers-Volume 2*, pages 193–197. Association for Computational Linguistics.

Ben Swanson. 2013. Exploring syntactic representations for native language identification. In *Proceedings of the Eighth Workshop on Innovative Use of NLP for Building Educational Applications*, pages 146–151.

Joel R Tetreault, Daniel Blanchard, Aoife Cahill, and Martin Chodorow. 2012. Native tongues, lost and found: Resources and empirical evaluations in native language identification. In *Proceedings of the 24th International Conference on Computational Linguistics*, pages 2585–2602.

Sze-Meng Jojo Wong and Mark Dras. 2011. Exploiting parse structures for native language identification. In *Proceedings of the Conference on Empirical Methods in Natural Language Processing*, pages 1600–1610. Association for Computational Linguistics.

Helen Yannakoudakis, Ted Briscoe, and Ben Medlock. 2011. A new dataset and method for automatically grading ESOL texts. In *Proceedings of the 49th Annual Meeting of the Association for Computational Linguistics: Human Language Technologies-Volume 1*, pages 180–189. Association for Computational Linguistics.

Challenging Learners in Their Individual Zone of Proximal Development Using Pedagogic Developmental Benchmarks of Syntactic Complexity

Xiaobin Chen and **Detmar Meurers**
LEAD Graduate School and Research Network
Department of Linguistics
Eberhard Karls Universität Tübingen, Germany
{xiaobin.chen,detmar.meurers}@uni-tuebingen.de

Abstract

This paper introduces an Intelligent Computer Assisted Language Learning system designed to provide reading input for language learners based on the syntactic complexity of their language production. The system analyzes the linguistic complexity of texts produced by the user and of texts in a pedagogic target language corpus to identify texts that are well-suited to foster acquisition. These texts provide developmental benchmarks offering an individually tailored language challenge, making ideas such as Krashen's i+1 or Vygotsky's Zone of Proximal Development concrete and empirically explorable in terms of a broad range of complexity measures in all dimensions of linguistic modeling.

1 Introduction

The analysis of linguistic complexity is a prominent endeavor in Second Language Acquisition (SLA) where Natural Language Processing (NLP) technologies are increasingly applied in a way broadening the empirical foundation. Automatic complexity analysis tools such as CohMetrix (McNamara et al., 2014), the L2 Syntactic Complexity Analyzer (Lu, 2010), and the Common Text Analysis Platform (Chen and Meurers, 2016) support studies analyzing interlanguage development (Lu, 2011; Lu and Ai, 2015; Mazgutova and Kormos, 2015), performance evaluation (Yang et al., 2015; Taguchi et al., 2013), and readability assessment (Vajjala and Meurers, 2012; Nelson et al., 2012).

In this paper, we introduce a new system called *Syntactic Benchmark (SyB)* that utilizes NLP to create syntactic complexity benchmarks

and identify reading material individually challenging learners, essentially instantiating the next stage of acquisition as captured by Krashen's concept of i+1 (Krashen, 1981) or relatedly, but emphasizing the social perspective, Vygotsky's Zone of Proximal Development (ZPD; Vygotsky, 1976).

In terms of structure of the paper, we first locate our approach in terms of the Complexity, Accuracy, and Fluency (CAF) framework in SLA research. Then we review approaches adopted by earlier studies in developmental complexity research, including problems they pose for a pedagogical approach aimed at offering developmental benchmarks. We propose and justify a solution, before presenting the architecture and functionality of the SyB system.

2 Development of Syntactic Complexity

The three-part model of development distinguishing Complexity, Accuracy, and Fluency has gained significant popularity among SLA researchers (Wolfe-Quintero et al., 1998; Skehan, 2009; Housen et al., 2009; Bulté and Housen, 2012) since it was first delineated by Skehan (1989). It provides SLA researchers with a systematic and quantitative approach to development. Among the CAF triplet, complexity arguably is the most researched and most "complex" due to its polysemous and multidimensional nature (Bulté and Housen, 2012; Vyatkina et al., 2015). Complexity in the SLA literature has been used to refer to task, cognitive, or linguistic complexity (Housen et al., 2009). In the present paper, we investigate complexity from a linguistic perspective, where it is concisely characterized by Ellis (2003) as "the extent to which language produced in performing a task is elaborate and varied". While the linguistic complexity construct consists of a range of sub-constructs at all levels of linguistic modeling, such as lexical, morphological, syntactic, semantic, pragmatic and discourse (Lu, 2010; Lu, 2011;

Xiaobin Chen and Detmar Meurers 2017. Challenging learners in their individual zone of proximal development using pedagogic developmental benchmarks of syntactic complexity. *Proceedings of the Joint 6th Workshop on NLP for Computer Assisted Language Learning and 2nd Workshop on NLP for Research on Language Acquisition at NoDaLiDa 2017.* Linköping Electronic Conference Proceedings 134: 8–17.

Lu and Ai, 2015; Ortega, 2015; Mazgutova and Kormos, 2015; Jarvis, 2013; Kyle and Crossley, 2015), the focus in this paper is on syntactic complexity.

In line with Ellis's (2003) definition of linguistic complexity, Ortega (2003) characterized syntactic complexity as the range of syntactic structures and the elaborateness or degree of sophistication of those structures in the language production, which we adopt as the operational definition in this paper. The uses of syntactic complexity analysis in SLA research include (i) gauging proficiency, (ii) assessing production quality, and (iii) benchmarking development (Ortega, 2012; Lu and Ai, 2015).

The development of syntactic complexity in language produced by learners is closely related to the learner's proficiency development. While the goal of language acquisition is not as such to produce complex language, advanced learners usually demonstrate the ability to understand and produce more complex language. With increasing proficiency, the learners are expanding their syntactic repertoire and capacity to use a wider range of linguistic resources offered by the given grammar (Ortega, 2015), thus producing "progressively more elaborate language" and "greater variety of syntactic patterning", constituting development in syntactic complexity (Foster and Skehan, 1996). As a result, syntactic complexity is often used to determine proficiency or assess performance in the target language (Larsen-Freeman, 1978; Ortega, 2003; Ortega, 2012; Vyatkina et al., 2015; Wolfe-Quintero et al., 1998; Lu, 2011; Taguchi et al., 2013; Yang et al., 2015; Sotillo, 2000).

Besides the practical side of performance assessment and placement, in SLA research the developmental perspective is considered to be "at the core of the phenomenon of L2 syntactic complexity" (Ortega, 2015). However, it is also the least addressed and understood phenomenon of syntactic complexity in SLA research (Vyatkina et al., 2015; Ortega, 2012). Understanding the development of syntactic complexity would enable SLA researchers to determine trajectories of the learners' development and set benchmarks for certain time points or across a given time span. On the practical side, such work could help language teachers select or design appropriate learning materials, and it can provide a reference frame for testing the effectiveness of instructional interventions. Hence researching syntactic complexity from a developmental perspective is of far-reaching relevance and applicability.

2.1 Development of Syntactic Complexity in Learner Corpora

A number of longitudinal and cross-sectional studies have been conducted to investigate the relationship between syntactic complexity and learner proficiency, aimed at finding (i) the most informative complexity measures across proficiency levels (Lu, 2011; Ferris, 1994; Ishikawa, 1995), (ii) the patterns of development for different syntactic measures (Bardovi-Harlig and Bofman, 1989; Henry, 1996; Larsen-Freeman, 1978; Lu, 2011), or (iii) discovering a developmental trajectory of syntactic complexity from the learner production (Ortega, 2000; Ortega, 2003; Vyatkina, 2013; Vyatkina et al., 2015).

With a few exceptions (Vyatkina, 2013; Tono, 2004), one thing these studies have in common is that they analyze the syntactic complexity development of learners based on their production. This seems natural since it investigates complexity development by analyzing the production of the developing entity, i.e., the learners. In principle, a longitudinal learner corpus with a continuous record of productions from individual learners over time would seem to enable us to determine the developmental trajectory and linguistic complexity benchmarks. However, this approach encounters some challenges that make it suboptimal for determining developmental benchmarks in practice.

First, the approach is dependent on learner corpora varying significantly on a number of parameters such as the learners' background, the tasks eliciting the production, and the instructional settings, etc. Significant effects of such factors on the syntactic complexity of learner writing have been identified in a number of studies (Ellis and Yuan, 2004; Lu, 2011; Ortega, 2003; Sotillo, 2000; Way et al., 2000; Yang et al., 2015; Alexopoulou et al., 2017). Consequently, the developmental patterns or benchmarks constructed from different learner corpora, elicited using different tasks, etc. are likely to vary or even contradict each other. For example, the correlation between subordination frequency and proficiency level have been found to be positive (Aarts and Granger, 1998; Granger and Rayson, 1998; Grant and Ginther, 2000), negative (Lu, 2011; Reid, 1992), or uncorrelated (Ferris,

1994; Kormos, 2011). It is difficult to build on such conflicting findings in practice.

Second, the NLP tools used for the automatic complexity analysis do not work equally well when applied to the language produced by learners at varied proficiency levels. Complexity analysis is currently performed using tools developed for different analysis needs (McNamara et al., 2014; Lu, 2010; Kyle and Crossley, 2015; Chen and Meurers, 2016). They enable fast and robust analysis of large corpora, in principle making the conclusions drawn from these analyses more powerful. However, analyzing learner data can pose significant challenges to the NLP components, which were usually developed for and tested on edited native language, as found in newspapers. While some NLP tools were shown to be quite reliable for analyzing the writing of learners at upper intermediate proficiency or higher (Lu, 2010; Lu, 2011), their robustness for lower-level writing or for some types of task (e.g., not providing reliable sentence delimiting punctuation) is questionable, requiring dedicated normalization steps and conceptual considerations (Meurers and Dickinson, 2017). This may well be why developmental profiling has rarely been done for learner language below upper-intermediate proficiency levels, as Ortega and Sinicrope (2008) observed. This currently limits the possibility of determining developmental benchmarks or trajectories across the full range of proficiency levels.

Last but not least, second language proficiency development is systematically affected by individual differences, making complexity research findings from learner data chaotic and hard to generalize. For example, Vyatkina et al. (2015) observed a "non-linear waxing and waning" (p. 28) for different modifier categories in a longitudinal learner corpus. Norrby and Håkansson (2007) identified four different types of morphosyntactic complexity development in a corpus of Swedish adult learner language, referred to as "the Careful", "the Thorough", "the Risk-taker", and "the Recycler". The analysis of morphological development in English L2 acquisition presented by Murakami (2013; 2016) also highlights the importance of accounting for individual variation in modeling L2 development. As a result, given the current state of affairs and without complex models integrating a range of factors, developmental benchmarks based on learner corpora are

of limited practical use for proficiency placement or performance assessment. Naturally this does not mean that research into developmental patterns based on learner corpora is not important or relevant for SLA. On the contrary, the dynamic and adaptive nature of language acquisition means that it is challenging and interesting to approach language development in a way accounting for individual differences (Larsen-Freeman, 2006; Verspoor et al., 2008; Verspoor et al., 2012), task effects (Alexopoulou et al., 2017), and other factors. For benchmarking and developmental tool development it is useful to look for a more stable data source though.

2.2 Developmental Benchmarks of Complexity in a Pedagogic Corpus

Considering the challenges just discussed, we explore the analysis of syntactic complexity in pedagogic language corpora compiled from well-edited target language (TL). A pedagogic TL corpus is a corpus "consisting of all the language a learner has been exposed to" (Hunston, 2002), or more realistically "a large enough and representative sample of the language, spoken and written, a learner has been or is likely to be exposed to via teaching material, either in the classroom or during self-study activities" (Meunier and Gouverneur, 2009). An optimal TL corpus for benchmarking syntactic complexity development would be one that includes texts targeting learners at any proficiency level, i.e., covering the full spectrum.

The advantages of a pedagogic corpus for developmental benchmarking are two-fold: First, pedagogic corpora can be constructed to exhibit a linear development of complexity measures, as shown by Vyatkina (2013) and confirmed here later. While the developmental trajectory in learner productions is "bumpy" and influenced by individual differences, task, and other factors discussed earlier, the pedagogic corpus can be written in a way targeting increased linguistic complexity. This is desirable if one wants the class to follow an instructional progression enriching grammatical forms in line with the pedagogic input they receive (Vyatkina, 2013). Pedagogically, it should be easier for language teachers to select instructional materials based on a linear benchmark of linguistic complexity, especially if one has evidence of the students' proficiency using that same scale.

Second, the problem of the NLP tools being

challenged by learner language, especially that of the low-proficiency learners, is avoided since pedagogic corpora contain texts with grammatically well-formed and edited articles. Considering the high accuracy of current NLP for such text material, the developmental benchmark constructed from a pedagogic corpus using automatic complexity analysis tools should be highly reliable. It should be acknowledged that no benchmarking system can avoid analyzing learner language if the system is used for proficiency placement purposes (unless additional, external language tests are used). However, complexity benchmarks constructed based on a TL corpus are more reliable than a comparison with a benchmark computed based on learner corpora. If the NLP tools fail to process the learner production to be compared to the benchmark because of grammar errors, resulting in placing the student on a lower level of the TL benchmark, the placement in a sense still is indicative of the aspect of the learner language that needs to be improved.

In sum, the above review suggests that a developmental perspective to syntactic complexity aimed at teaching practice can be meaningfully approached with the assistance of a pedagogic corpus consisting of texts targeting learners in a wide spectrum of language proficiency. In the following section, we will introduce an NLP-based system based on this idea.

3 The Syntactic Benchmark System

Syntactic Benchmark (SyB) is an Intelligent Computer Assisted Language Learning (ICALL) system that analyzes the syntactic complexity of a text produced by a learner and places the text onto a developmental scale constructed from a comprehensive pedagogic corpus. The system aims at helping learners place the syntactic complexity level of their writings with regard to the pedagogic benchmark and identify the syntactic areas where further improvement is needed. The system is able to visualize the developmental benchmark for different syntactic complexity measures and the learner's position on the benchmark for the selected complexity index. Based on the complexity level of the user's language output, SyB then proposes appropriately challenging texts from the pedagogic corpus. Reading these texts providing "i+1" input should help the user advance in language proficiency. The size of the "+1", i.e., the degree of

the challenge and the overall proficiency level that the learner assumes being at currently are manually specified by the user.

Figure 1 shows the Data Window, into which the learner enters a text they wrote to identify its level in terms of syntactic complexity in relation to the TL benchmark corpus. In Figure 2, we see the Visualization Window providing the result of the analysis for the selected complexity feature (here, the Mean Length of Clause measure). The boxplots show the results for each text in each level in the TL benchmark corpus, and a red line indicates the measure's value for the learner text. Selecting the "Challenge" button leads to the Search Result Window shown in Figure 3. It provides a search result list with links to TL articles intended as i+1 input material for the learner. The texts are slightly above the level of the learner text in terms of the selected complexity measure, with the degree of the challenge being determined by the user setting. The learner also specifies the overall proficiency level they assume to be in so that the text challenging them in terms of the selected complexity measure is selected from the pool of texts intended for that overall proficiency level.

In the following, we take a closer look at the SyB components.

3.1 The Pedagogic Corpus

The pedagogic TL corpus used for constructing the syntactic complexity benchmark consists of 14,581 news articles from the educational website Newsela[1], which is a website that provides news articles on a wide range of topics. Each article on the website is adapted into five reading levels (including an "original" level, which is the article in its unadapted form) by human editors. Newsela uses the Lexile Framework (Lexile, 2007) for text leveling and provides a grade to Lexile mapping for converting from Lexile scores to US grade levels. Since the grade level is easier to understand for most users, the SyB system uses grade levels as benchmarking levels. For copyright reasons, the SyB system does not store the original articles from Newsela. It only keeps records of the complexity statistics of the articles and the Search Result Window provides the results in terms of links to the text on the Newsela web site.

---

[1]https://newsela.com

Proceedings of the Joint 6th Workshop on NLP for Computer Assisted Language Learning and 2nd Workshop on NLP for Research on Language Acquisition at NoDaLiDa 2017

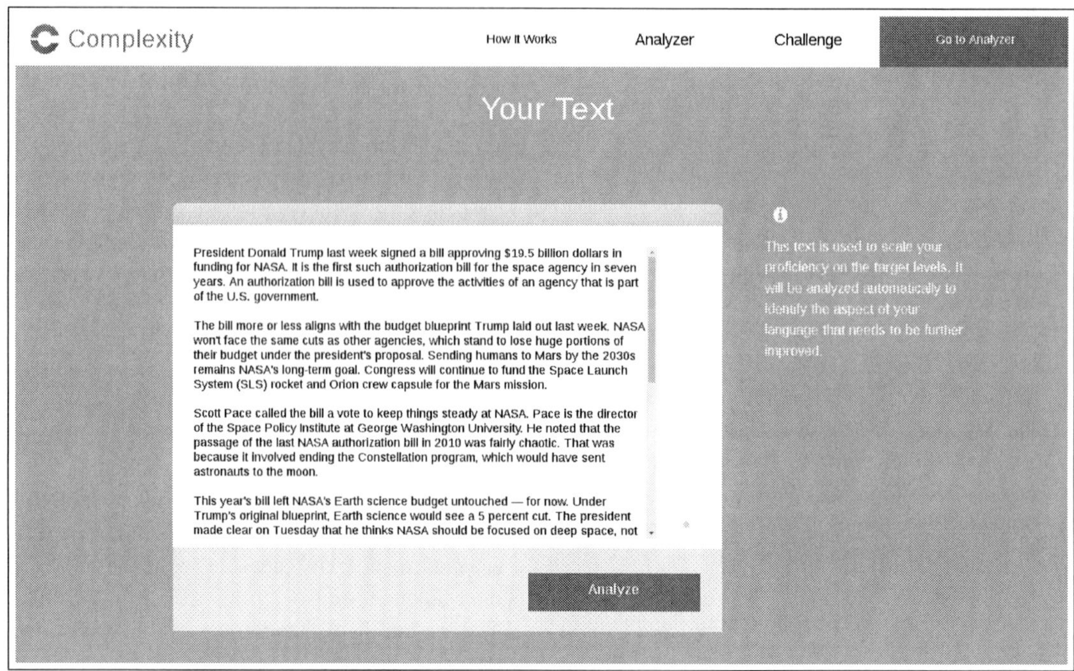

Figure 1: The Data Window of the Syntactic Benchmark Analyzer, where users can paste a composition to identify their level in relation to the TL benchmark corpus

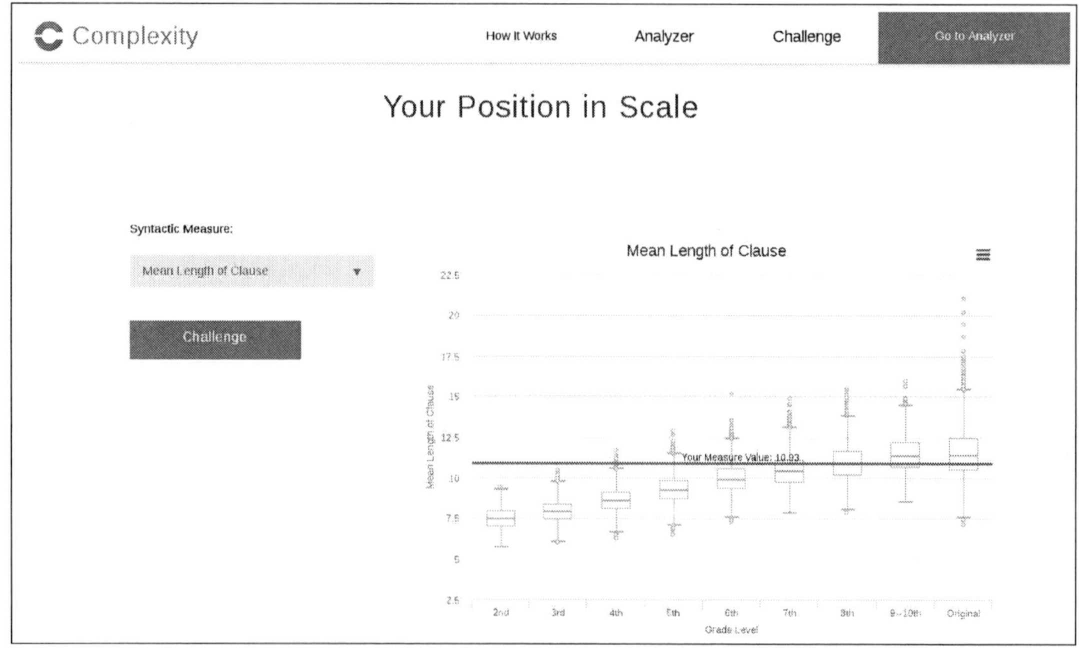

Figure 2: The Visualization Window showing the users' level (red line) for the selected syntactic complexity measure (here: Mean Length of Clause) in relation to the TL benchmark corpus

Figure 3: The Search Result Window supporting selection of TL articles based on the learner production's syntactic complexity level (and user-specified degree of challenge and overall target grade level)

3.2 NLP Processing

Each article in the Newsela TL reading corpus was processed with an NLP pipeline consisting of a sentence segmenter, a tokenizer and a parser from the Stanford CoreNLP Toolkit library (Manning et al., 2014). Tregex (Levy and Andrew, 2006), a utility for tree pattern matching, was used to extract syntactic units such as coordinate phrases, clauses, and T-units from the parse tree of a sentence.

We used the Tregex patterns of Lu's (2010) L2 Syntactic Complexity Analyzer and calculated the same set of 14 syntactic indices suggested in his study (p. 479, Table 1). This set of syntactic features have also been used in developmental syntactic complexity studies and proved to be valid and reliable (Larsen-Freeman, 1978; Ortega, 2003; Wolfe-Quintero et al., 1998). The SyB system currently uses a replication of Lu's processing pipeline, which was shown to have achieved a very high level of reliability in a number of studies (Lu, 2010; Lu and Ai, 2015; Yang et al., 2015; Ai and Lu, 2013; Lu, 2011).

In future work, we plan to integrate the broad range of linguistic complexity measures offered by our Common Text Analysis Platform (Chen and Meurers, 2016).

3.3 Benchmarking and Challenging

For each of the 14 syntactic measures, a benchmark box plot of the measure values by grade level was created. Whenever the user pastes or enters a representative production and chooses the measure they are interested in, the SyB system calculates the chosen measure value from the user text and draws a horizontal red line across the benchmark box plot to signify the relative position of the user text's complexity level on the TL corpus benchmark. Figure 2 shows an example of a benchmark plot and the learner text as measured by the same complexity index, Mean Length of Clause.

The system then selects from the TL corpus those articles that challenge the user in terms of specific syntactic complexity as measured by the user's choice of complexity indicator. The user is also given choices of the overall target grade levels of the texts and the level of challenge they want to receive (Figure 3). The range of challenge levels matches the range of the syntactic measure calculated from the TL corpus. The complete challenge range is divided into ten sections and controlled by a range slider with those steps, shown as the red slider in the top-right corner of Figure 3.

Each article in the Newsela TL reading corpus

Proceedings of the Joint 6th Workshop on NLP for Computer Assisted Language Learning and 2nd Workshop on NLP for Research on Language Acquisition at NoDaLiDa 2017

comes with the overall evaluation of reading level by the editors. Since there is significant overlap in the range of complexity measure values across target reading levels, it is useful to let the user determine the overall pool of texts that they want the system to select from using the selected complexity measure. In SyB, the overall reading level of the challenge texts is selected using the drop-down listbox in the top-left corner of Figure 3. The current system then only evaluates a single complexity feature of the learner's production (in the case of Figure 2, Mean Length of Clauses) and proposes texts at an appropriately challenging levels based on this single aspect, selected from the pool of texts at the user-selected overall level.

This is not optimal because whether a text poses challenges to specific readers also depend on other factors, such as the lexical complexity, the learners' language competence including aspects such as strategic competence, their world and domain knowledge, and so forth. An alternative method we intend to explore in the future is to compute a broad range of complexity measures using the NLP from our Common Text Analysis Platform (Chen and Meurers, 2016) so that each text is represented by a vector encoding the results for each complexity measure for that text (which could also include dimensions for other factors to be considered, such as measures of the user's domain knowledge for different topics or subject domains). The overall i+1 challenge can then be computed using a vector distance metric (Manhattan, Euclidean, etc.). Perhaps most attractively, one could combine the two approaches, with the vector-based overall comparison replacing the current manual setting of the global level determining the set of texts to be considered, and the challenge being determined by the user-selected single complexity measure as in the current approach.

The hypothesis behind the overall setup is that by reading the challenging texts, the users will "align" (Wang and Wang, 2015) to the target levels of syntactic complexity, hence promoting their TL proficiency. Whether this hypothesis is correct and which approach works best for determining input material appropriately challenging learners is an empirical question. Answering it should also provide important insights into the question how Krashen's notion of an i+1 (or Vygotsky's ZPD) can be operationalized in terms of measurable features such as linguistic complexity.

4 Summary and Outlook

This paper introduced the ICALL system SyB for benchmarking syntactic complexity development based on a TL corpus. A TL corpus can provide a consistent, linear, and complete instantiation of incremental complexification for different aspects of linguistic complexity. Current NLP technologies are more robust for analyzing such TL corpora than for analyzing learner corpora. As a result, syntactic complexity benchmarks in TL corpora may be more applicable and relevant for instructional use than models of linguistic complexification based on learner corpora, which are harder to analyze automatically, exhibit significant individual variation, task effects, and other uncontrolled factors. However, this hypothesis remains to be validated empirically in actual teaching practice. Future research also needs to investigate which level of challenge for which of the complexity measures at which domain of linguistic modeling is most effective at fostering learning, i.e., what constitutes the best +1 for which aspect of linguistic complexity (for learners with which individual characteristics). Last but not least, while the SyB system provides users with options to control the syntactic complexity and overall reading challenge levels, the system does not take into account the gap between the active ability exhibited in production and the passive ability used for comprehension. The receptive and productive knowledge were found to differ within learners in a number of studies (Zhong, 2016; Schmitt and Redwood, 2011).

We plan to empirically evaluate the system's effectiveness in providing input individually tailored to the i+1 in terms of linguistic complexity as a means to foster learning. It will also be interesting to compare this kind of individual adaptation of the complexity of the input based on the complexity analysis of the learner's production with the input enrichment supported by a teacher-based selection of the constructions targeted to be learned as supported by the FLAIR system (Chinkina and Meurers, 2016).

Finally, it will be interesting to enhance the system by making the texts it suggests for reading adaptive not only to what the learner is capable of producing, but also to how well the learner understands the articles suggested by the system. We are currently developing a production task module where the learner is asked to produce output af-

Proceedings of the Joint 6th Workshop on NLP for Computer Assisted Language Learning and 2nd Workshop on NLP for Research on Language Acquisition at NoDaLiDa 2017

ter reading the complexity challenge texts. This will make it possible to analyze (i) whether there is uptake of the increasingly complex language being read and (ii) how the complexification impacts the user's comprehension of the challenging texts. In principle, the system could then be extended to adapt the subsequent text challenges based on a combination of these form and meaning factors.

Acknowledgments

This research was funded by the LEAD Graduate School & Research Network [GSC1028], a project of the Excellence Initiative of the German federal and state governments. Xiaobin Chen is a doctoral student at the LEAD Graduate School & Research Network.

References

Jan Aarts and Sylviane Granger. 1998. Tag sequences in learner corpora: a key to interlanguage grammar and discourse. In Sylviane Granger, editor, *Learner English on Computer*, pages 132–141. Longman, London; New York.

Haiyang Ai and Xiaofei Lu. 2013. A corpus-based comparison of syntactic complexity in NNS and NS university students' writing. In Ana Daz-Negrillo, Nicolas Ballier, and Paul Thompson, editors, *Automatic Treatment and Analysis of Learner Corpus Data*, pages 249–264. John Benjamins.

Theodora Alexopoulou, Marije Michel, Akira Murakami, and Detmar Meurers. 2017. Analyzing learner language in task contexts: A study case of task-based performance in EFCAMDAT. *Language Learning*. Special Issue on "Language learning research at the intersection of experimental, corpusbased and computational methods: Evidence and interpretation".

Kathleen Bardovi-Harlig and Theodora Bofman. 1989. Attainment of syntactic and morphological accuracy by advanced language learners. *Studies in Second Language Acquisition*, 11(1):17–34.

Bram Bulté and Alex Housen. 2012. Defining and operationalising l2 complexity. In Alex Housen, Folkert Kuiken, and Ineke Vedder, editors, *Dimensions of L2 Performance and Proficiency*, pages 21–46. John Benjamins.

Xiaobin Chen and Detmar Meurers. 2016. CTAP: A web-based tool supporting automatic complexity analysis. In *Proceedings of the Workshop on Computational Linguistics for Linguistic Complexity*, Osaka, Japan, December. The International Committee on Computational Linguistics.

Maria Chinkina and Detmar Meurers. 2016. Linguistically-aware information retrieval: Providing input enrichment for second language learners. In *Proceedings of the 11th Workshop on Innovative Use of NLP for Building Educational Applications*, pages 188–198, San Diego, CA.

Rod Ellis and Fangyuan Yuan. 2004. The effects of planning on fluency, complexity, and accuracy in second language narrative writing. *Studies in Second Language Acquisition*, 26(1):59–84.

Rod Ellis. 2003. *Task-based Language Learning and Teaching*. Oxford University Press, Oxford, UK.

Dana R. Ferris. 1994. Lexical and syntactic features of esl writing by students at different levels of l2 proficiency. *TESOL Quarterly*, 28(2):414–420.

Pauline Foster and Peter Skehan. 1996. The influence of planning and task type on second language performance. *Studies in Second Language Acquisition*, 18(3):299–323.

Sylviane Granger and Paul Rayson. 1998. Automatic profiling of learner texts. In Sylviane Granger, editor, *Learner English on Computer*, pages 119–131. Longman, New York.

Leslie Grant and April Ginther. 2000. Using computer-tagged linguistic features to describe L2 writing differences. *Journal of Second Language Writing*, 9(2):123–145.

Kathryn Henry. 1996. Early l2 writing development: A study of autobiographical essays by university-level students of russian. *The Modern Language Journal*, 80(3):309–326.

Alex Housen, Folkert Kuiken, Jane Zuengler, and Ken Hyland. 2009. Complexity, accuracy and fluency in second language acquisition. *Applied Linguistics*, 30(4):461–473.

Susan Hunston. 2002. *Corpora in Applied Linguistics*. Cambridge University Press.

Sandra Ishikawa. 1995. Objective measurement of low-proficiency efl narrative writing. *Journal of Second Language Writing*, 4(1):51 – 69.

Scott Jarvis. 2013. Capturing the diversity in lexical diversity. *Language Learning*, 63:87–106.

Judit Kormos. 2011. Task complexity and linguistic and discourse features of narrative writing performance. *Journal of Second Language Writing*, 20(2):148 – 161.

Stephen D. Krashen. 1981. The fundamental pedagogical principle in second language teaching. *Studia Linguistica*, 35(1–2):50–70, December.

Kristopher Kyle and Scott A Crossley. 2015. Automatically assessing lexical sophistication: Indices, tools, findings, and application. *TESOL Quarterly*, 49(4):757–786.

Diane Larsen-Freeman. 1978. An ESL index of development. *TESOL Quarterly*, 12(4):439–448.

Diane Larsen-Freeman. 2006. The emergence of complexity, fluency, and accuracy in the oral and written production of five chinese learners of english. *Applied Linguistics*, 27(4):590–619.

Roger Levy and Galen Andrew. 2006. Tregex and tsurgeon: tools for querying and manipulating tree data structures. In *5th International Conference on Language Resources and Evaluation*, Genoa, Italy.

Lexile. 2007. The Lexile Framework® for reading: Theoretical framework and development. Technical report, MetaMetrics, Inc., Durham, NC.

Xiaofei Lu and Haiyang Ai. 2015. Syntactic complexity in college-level English writing: Differences among writers with diverse l1 backgrounds. *Journal of Second Language Writing*, -:in press.

Xiaofei Lu. 2010. Automatic analysis of syntactic complexity in second language writing. *International Journal of Corpus Linguistics*, 15(4):474–496.

Xiaofei Lu. 2011. A corpus-based evaluation of syntactic complexity measures as indices of college-level esl writers' language development. *TESOL Quarterly*, 45(1):36–62, March.

Christopher D. Manning, Mihai Surdeanu, John Bauer, Jenny Finkel, Steven J. Bethard, and David McClosky. 2014. The Stanford CoreNLP natural language processing toolkit. In *Association for Computational Linguistics (ACL) System Demonstrations*, pages 55–60.

Diana Mazgutova and Judit Kormos. 2015. Syntactic and lexical development in an intensive english for academic purposes programme. *Journal of Second Language Writing*, 29:3–15.

Danielle A. McNamara, Arthur C. Graesser, Philip M. McCarthy, and Zhiqiang Cai. 2014. *Automated evaluation of text and discourse with Coh-Metrix*. Cambridge University Press, Cambridge, M.A.

Fanny Meunier and Céline Gouverneur. 2009. New types of corpora for new educational challenges: Collecting, annotating and exploiting a corpus of textbook material. In Karin Aijmer, editor, *Corpora and Language Teaching*, pages 179–201. John Benjamins, Amsterdam.

Detmar Meurers and Markus Dickinson. 2017. Evidence and interpretation in language learning research: Opportunities for collaboration with computational linguistics. *Language Learning*, 67(2). http://dx.doi.org/10.1111/lang.12233.

Akira Murakami. 2013. *Individual Variation and the Role of L1 in the L2 Development of English Grammatical Morphemes: Insights From Learner Corpora*. Ph.D. thesis, University of Cambridge.

Akira Murakami. 2016. Modeling systematicity and individuality in nonlinear second language development: The case of english grammatical morphemes. *Language Learning*, 6(4):834–871.

Jessica Nelson, Charles Perfetti, David Liben, and Meredith Liben. 2012. Measures of text difficulty: Testing their predictive value for grade levels and student performance. Technical report, The Council of Chief State School Officers.

Catrin Norrby and Gisela Håkansson. 2007. The interaction of complexity and grammatical processability: The case of swedish as a foreign language. *International Review of Applied Linguistics in Language Teaching*, 45:45–68.

Lourdes Ortega and C. Sinicrope. 2008. Novice proficiency in a foreign language: A study of task-based performance profiling on the STAMP test. Technical report, Center for Applied Second Language Studies, University of Oregon.

Lourdes Ortega. 2000. *Understanding syntactic complexity: The measurement of change in the syntax of instructed L2 Spanish learners*. Unpublished doctoral dissertation, University of Hawaii, Manoa, HI.

Lourdes Ortega. 2003. Syntactic complexity measures and their relationship to L2 proficiency: A research synthesis of college-level L2 writing. *Applied Linguistics*, 24(4):492–518.

Lourdes Ortega. 2012. A construct in search of theoretical renewal. In B. Szmrecsanyi and B. Kortmann, editors, *Linguistic complexity: Second language acquisition, indigenization, contact*, pages 127–155. de Gruyter, Berlin.

Lourdes Ortega. 2015. Syntactic complexity in l2 writing: Progress and expansion. *Journal of Second Language Writing*, 29:82–94.

Joy Reid. 1992. A computer text analysis of four cohesion devices in english discourse by native and non-native writers. *Journal of Second Language Writing*, 1(2):79–107.

Norbert Schmitt and Stephen Redwood. 2011. Learner knowledge of phrasal verbs: A corpus-informed study. In Fanny Meunier, Sylvie De Cock, Gaëtanelle Gilquin, and Magali Paquot, editors, *A Taste for Corpora. In Honour of Sylviane Granger*, pages 173–207. John Benjamins Publishing Company, Amsterdam.

Peter Skehan. 1989. *Individual Differences in Second Language Learning*. Edward Arnold.

Peter Skehan. 2009. Modelling second language performance: Integrating complexity, accuracy, fluency, and lexis. *Applied Linguistics*, 30(4):510–532.

Susana M. Sotillo. 2000. Discourse functions and syntactic complexity in synchronous and asynchronous communication. *Language Learning & Technology*, 4(1):82–119.

Naoko Taguchi, William Crawford, and Danielle Zawodny Wetzel. 2013. What linguistic features are indicative of writing quality? a case of argumentative essays in a college composition program. *TESOL Quarterly*, 47(2):420–430.

Yukio Tono. 2004. Multiple comparisons of IL, L1 and TL corpora: the case of L2 acquisition of verb subcategorization patterns by Japanese learners of English. In Guy Aston, Silvia Bernardini, and Dominic Stewart, editors, *Corpora and Language Learners*, pages 45–66. John Benjamins.

Sowmya Vajjala and Detmar Meurers. 2012. On improving the accuracy of readability classification using insights from second language acquisition. In Joel Tetreault, Jill Burstein, and Claudial Leacock, editors, *In Proceedings of the 7th Workshop on Innovative Use of NLP for Building Educational Applications*, pages 163–173, Montral, Canada, June. Association for Computational Linguistics.

Marjolijn Verspoor, Wander Lowie, and Marijn Van Dijk. 2008. Variability in second language development from a dynamic systems perspective. *The Modern Language Journal*, 92(2):214–231.

Marjolijn Verspoor, Monika S. Schmid, and Xiaoyan Xu. 2012. A dynamic usage based perspective on L2 writing. *Journal of Second Language Writing*, 21(3):239–263.

Nina Vyatkina, Hagen Hirschmann, and Felix Golcher. 2015. Syntactic modification at early stages of L2 german writing development: A longitudinal learner corpus study. *Journal of Second Language Writing*, 29:28–50.

Nina Vyatkina. 2013. Specific syntactic complexity: Developmental profiling of individuals based on an annotated learner corpus. *The Modern Language Journal*, 97(S1):11–30.

Lev Semenovich Vygotsky. 1986. *Thought and Language*. MIT Press, Cambridge, MA.

Chuming Wang and Min Wang. 2015. Effect of alignment on l2 written production. *Applied Linguistics*, 36(5).

Denise Paige Way, Elizabeth G. Joiner, and Michael A. Seaman. 2000. Writing in the secondary foreign language classroom: The effects of prompts and tasks on novice learners of french. *The Modern Language Journal*, 84(2):171–184.

Kate Wolfe-Quintero, Shunji Inagaki, and Hae-Young Kim. 1998. *Second Language Development in Writing: Measures of Fluency, Accuracy & Complexity*. Second Language Teaching & Curriculum Center, University of Hawaii at Manoa, Honolulu.

Weiwei Yang, Xiaofei Lu, and Sara Cushing Weigle. 2015. Different topics, different discourse: Relationships among writing topic, measures of syntactic complexity, and judgments of writing quality. *Journal of Second Language Writing*, 28:53–67.

Hua Flora Zhong. 2016. The relationship between receptive and productive vocabulary knowledge: a perspective from vocabulary use in sentence writing. *The Language Learning Journal*, Advanced Access.

Crossing the Border Twice: Reimporting Prepositions to Alleviate L1-Specific Transfer Errors

Johannes Graën
Institute of Computational Linguistics
University of Zurich
graen@cl.uzh.ch

Gerold Schneider
Institute of Computational Linguistics
University of Zurich
gschneid@cl.uzh.ch

Abstract

We present a data-driven approach which exploits word alignment in a large parallel corpus with the objective of identifying those verb- and adjective-preposition combinations which are difficult for L2 language learners. This allows us, on the one hand, to provide language-specific ranked lists in order to help learners to focus on particularly challenging combinations given their native language (L1). On the other hand, we provide extensive statistics on such combinations with the objective of facilitating automatic error correction for preposition use in learner texts. We evaluate these lists, first manually, and secondly automatically by applying our statistics to an error-correction task.

1 Introduction

Computational Linguistics and Learner Error research have made impressive progress recently, but they have not reached their collaborative potential yet (Granger and Lefer 2016, p. 281). For example, while language teaching materials contain lists of idioms and phrasal verbs, the decision for which items to include often does not take actual frequency of use or particular difficulties for learners with specific backgrounds into account.

The current paper addresses this shortcoming, by exploiting large parallel and error-annotated learner corpora. We focus on verb-preposition combinations (VPC), including phrasal verbs and adjective-preposition combinations (APC) obtained from a large parallel corpus (Europarl). For brevity's sake we only describe VPC here.

Our aim is to provide practical and customized help to the learner of a language, here English, by pointing out errors that are likely to be made and to correct them where they occur. In particular, we provide a) a list of VPC/APC that vary considerably between languages, b) a list of specific VPC/APC errors that are to be expected from a native speaker of a particular language, and c) a resource which detects probably incorrect VPC/APC uses and suggests a correction. Concerning c), advances have been made recently due to the CoNLL shared tasks on grammatical error correction (Ng, M. S. Wu, Y. Wu, et al. 2013; Ng, M. S. Wu, Briscoe, et al. 2014), and due to systems targeting preposition errors (Tetreault and Chodorow 2008; Boyd et al. 2012). We evaluate our results on ICLE (Granger, Dagneaux, et al. 2002), the FCE dataset (Yannakoudakis et al. 2011), and the NICT Japanese Learner English Corpus[1]. Furthermore, we exploit ICLE in combination with the British National Corpus (BNC) (Aston and Burnard 1998) to attain collocation statistics which allow us to evaluate the proposed suggestions for corrections.

Non-standard uses by language learners, which we refer to as errors here, can be found at any linguistic level. Some errors can be detected easily by current word-processing tools (e.g. spelling errors) or by re-reading, or consulting dictionaries. But particularly in areas where grammar and lexis interact, there is typically a lack of tools.

One frequent source of lexico-grammatical errors are VPC. While semantically transparent prepositions (e.g. *stand on*) are relatively stable cross-linguistically, the frequent nonsemantic prepositions (e.g. *wait for*) and phrasal verbs (e.g. *depend on*) show enormous cross-linguistic variation. VPC are difficult to acquire for language learners (Gilquin, Granger, et al. 2011, pp. 59–60). Phrasal verbs represent "one of the most notoriously challenging aspects of English language instruction" (Gardner and Davies 2007, p. 339; see

[1] https://alaginrc.nict.go.jp/nict_jle/ index_E.html

Johannes Graën and Gerold Schneider 2017. Crossing the border twice: Reimporting prepositions to alleviate L1-specific transfer errors. *Proceedings of the Joint 6th Workshop on NLP for Computer Assisted Language Learning and 2nd Workshop on NLP for Research on Language Acquisition at NoDaLiDa 2017.* Linköping Electronic Conference Proceedings 134: 18–26.

also Gilquin 2015). In the CoNLL shared tasks, prepositional errors were the third most frequent error type at 5 to 9 % of all errors (only determiner errors and noun number are more frequent). We include APC as they are often similarly difficult to acquire for learners of English. Benson et al. (2009) recognize APC as an independent category in addition to VPC.

2 Corpus Preparation

We extracted parallel text units in English, Finnish, French, German, Italian, Polish and Spanish from the *Corrected & Structured Europarl Corpus (CoStEP)* (Graën et al. 2014) which is a cleaned version of the Europarl Corpus (Koehn 2005).

We identified approximately 40 million tokens in five languages: English, French, German, Italian and Spanish. Finnish and Polish have considerable fewer tokens than the other languages (30 million and 10 million, respectively).[2]

2.1 Tagging and Lemmatization

For tagging and lemmatization, we used *TreeTagger* (Schmid 1994). To increase tagging accuracy for words unknown to the language model, we had to extend the tagging lexica, especially the German one, with lemmas and part-of-speech tags for frequent words. Moreover, we used the word alignment information between the languages (see below) to disambiguate lemmas for those tokens where the TreeTagger provided multiple lemmatization options.[3]

2.2 Alignment

On the sentence segments identified (about 1.7 million per language), we performed pairwise sentence alignment with *hunalign* (Varga et al. 2005) and based on that word alignment with *GIZA++* (Och and Ney 2003; Gao and Vogel 2008) and the Berkeley Aligner (Liang et al. 2006). While the Berkeley Aligner computes bidirectional word alignments, the alignments of GIZA++ are unidirectional and thus need to be symmetrized if bidirectional alignments are required. We chose the

union symmetrization method since it increases recall. Word alignment was performed on the types of all tokens and on lemmas of content words.[4] For the latter, we mapped the individual tag sets to the universal tagset defined by Petrov et al. (2012) and defined content words to be those tokens being tagged as nouns, verbs, adjectives or adverbs.

2.3 Parsing

We used *MaltParser* (Nivre et al. 2006) to derive syntactic dependency relations in English. For parsing our tagged texts, we had to map several part-of-speech tags beforehand as the standard English parameter file distributed with *TreeTagger* slightly differs.[5]

3 Methods

In the following, we first present our concept of backtranslating prepositions based on automatic annotation and alignment frequencies. We then apply it to VPC and introduce our method for error correction.

3.1 Distributions

In a first step, we calculate a lemma distribution matrix by aggregating lemma counts on token alignments. This matrix tells us the translation ratio of each lemma. Each cell contains the probability of a lemma in the source language to be translated into a lemma in the foreign language. For example, the English verb *suffer* is translated to German *leiden* in 42 % of the cases.

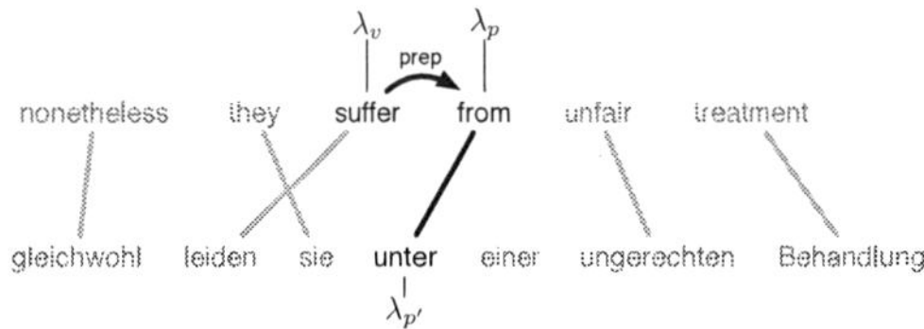

Figure 1: Corpus example: first, the VPC is identified employing syntactic dependency relations, second, the foreign language preposition of the VPC is retrieved following the word alignment.

We then retrieve the set of all English VPC (consisting of verb λ_v and preposition λ_p with the verb showing a syntactic 'preposition' relation to the preposition as depicted in Fig. 1) and calculate the

---

[2]For Polish this is due to the fact that Poland joined the European Union in 2004 and translations for the debates are only available from 2006 onwards. In case of Finnish, the gap can be explained by the language itself which features a rich morphology, thus resulting in less tokens at the expense of more word forms.

[3]The disambiguation approach is similar to the one Volk et al. (2016) describe, except that we combine alignment information for all languages simultaneously.

[4]If no lemma provided we used the word form instead.

[5]It distinguishes e.g. between main and auxiliary verbs, and between prepositions and complementizers.

distribution of observed prepositions. For example, the English verb *suffer* occurs with the preposition *from* in 26 % of all cases, but also, more rarely, with other prepositions.[6] We do not attempt to make a distinction between phrasal verbs, PP complements or PP adjuncts in our data-driven approach.

For each VPC, we count the foreign prepositions $\lambda_{p'}$ as they are aligned with the source VPC's prepositions λ_p.[7] We do this step for each language separately.

λ_v	λ_p	$\lambda_{p''}$	BTS	BTR
suffer	from	under	102.512	2.51
suffer	from	of	100.036	2.46
suffer	from	in	78.559	1.93
suffer	from	by	51.188	1.25
suffer	from	on	46.534	1.14
suffer	from	**from**	**40.966**	**1.00**
suffer	from	with	36.322	0.89
suffer	from	among	27.927	0.68
suffer	from	at	15.791	0.39
suffer	from	amongst	11.207	0.28
		$\vdots$		

Table 1: Backtranslation score (BTS) and backtranslation ratio (BTR) for different backtranslated prepositions ($\lambda_{p''}$) of *suffer from*.

3.2 Backtranslation Score (BTS)

By multiplying these foreign prepositions with the lemma distribution matrix, we obtain a list of English prepositions and values that we call backtranslation score (BTS). BTS tells us how preferred a certain source language preposition is[8] for a foreign language, given a particular VPC.

3.3 Backtranslation Ratio (BTR)

We then normalize BTS to what we refer to as backtranslation ratio (BTR), such that the BTR of the correct English preposition for a particular verb and language is 1.0, i.e. each preposition's BTS divided by the BTS of the correct original preposition, which is shown in Table 1. A BTR above 1.0 indicates that it is more likely to choose a wrong preposition than the correct one, according to our language model, which is based on alignment (see Appendix for the most likely incorrect preposition per language, with their BTR).

The BTR calculated for English VPC give us an impression of how difficult the preposition of a particular expression would be for a speaker of the respective language. For instance, the highest BTR for the verb *aim* is 2.74 for German (preposition *on*, presumably due to German *zielen auf*) and 2.81 for French (preposition *in*, indirectly due to French *viser* + object, see next subsection) while *at* is 1.0 by definition.

We also include the raw frequency of VPC and derive the final ranking for each VPC and language based on both normalized scores.[9] For space reasons, we only present the intersection of all language specific VPC and APC lists in Table 2.

3.4 Suggestions for Corrections

In addition to lists of difficult VPC and APC, we also suggest a correction for incorrect combinations based on the distribution of prepositions retrieved. Errors can be simple misproductions such as typos or copy-paste errors, which are typically spotted when carefully re-reading a text. But when speakers of certain linguistic backgrounds keep producing the same non-standard form repeatedly, often due to native language influence such as transfer, they make errors which are more difficult to detect for them, and thus a resource which spots these is particularly helpful. These errors follow a repeated pattern, often reaching collocational status. Schneider and Gilquin (2016) use collocation-based statistics to detect such non-standard VPC by measuring the expected (E) collocational strength in Learner English (based on the International Corpus of Learner English (ICLE)), compared to the observed (O) collocational strength in native English (based on the BNC).

$$\text{O/E-ratio} = \frac{\text{O/E(ICLE)}}{\text{O/E(BNC)}} \quad (1)$$

We detect VPC errors following the same method, then address the question if we can provide the appropriate correction. Given an incorrect VPC, we suggest the most likely preposition, given the verb. As some errors involve a preposition instead of a direct object, our algorithm suggests to

---

[6] The second most frequent preposition together with *suffer* is *in*, occurring in 9 %. In 2 %, *suffer* is modified by a PP headed by *under*.

[7] We only consider alignments from English prepositions to prepositions in other languages.

[8] As we multiply by the entire lemma distribution matrix, this could theoretically also be other words than prepositions, but in practice only the prepositions count here.

[9] We calculate the same measures for APC analogously.

VERB/ADJ	PREP	OK?	I	N	F
aim	at	yes	+		
arrive	at	yes	+	+	+
benefit	from	yes	+		
breathe	into	?	*n/a*		
channel	into	yes	*n/a*		
complain	about	yes	+	+	+
compliment	on	yes			
convert	into	yes	*n/a*		
depend	on	yes	+		+
direct	at	yes	+		
divide	into	?	*n/a*		
emanate	from	yes			
embark	on	yes			
enter	into	?	*n/a*		
estimate	at	yes	+		
exclude	from	yes	+		
exempt	from	yes	+		
fall	within	yes			
force	into	yes	*n/a*		
gain	from	yes	+		
hang	over	no	*n/a*		
incorporate	into	?	*n/a*		
integrate	into	?	*n/a*		
level	at	no	*n/a*		
look	at	yes	+	+	+
miss	from	yes			
plunge	into	?	*n/a*		
preside	over	yes			
profit	from	yes	+		
protect	from	yes			
recover	from	yes			
suffer	from	yes			+
talk	about	yes	+	+	+
target	at	yes	+		
throw	into	?	*n/a*		
transform	into	?	*n/a*		
translate	into	?	*n/a*		
transpose	into	?	*n/a*		
wait	for	yes	+	+	+
worry	about	yes			+
absent	from	yes		+	
conditional	on	yes		+	
dependent	on	yes	+	+	+
early	as	no	*n/a*		
exempt	from	yes	+		
sceptical	about	yes	+		
serious	about	yes	+		
Total		34/10/3	23/31		

Table 2: Language-independent VPC/APC obtained by intersecting the language-specific recommendation lists. 23 out of 31 relevant ones can be found in at least one of the learner corpora we searched (I = ICLE; N = NICT; F = FCE).

use a direct object if the raw frequency of a verb is at least twice as high as the number of VPC involving that verb.

4 Results

In the following, we present results for all three aims identified above.

As we cannot give the full lists of recommended language-specific lists here,[10] we will focus instead on three verb-preposition combinations that are particularly useful to concentrate on and to learn for native speakers of German:

- *suffer from*: corresponds to German *leiden unter*, the preposition 'unter' directly translates as 'under'.
- *wait for*: corresponds to German *warten auf*, 'auf' directly translates as 'on'.
- *consist of*: corresponds to German *bestehen aus*, 'aus' directly translates as 'from'.

The recommended lists overlap, yet also differ considerably between languages. The amount of overlapping VPC of the whole lists ranges from 58 % for German-Polish to 97 % for French-Italian, reflecting the typological similarity of the languages. We consider those items that occur in each of the 5 language-specific lists as generally hard to learn. This language-independent list is given in Table 2.

The list of the top true positives, i.e. the correct suggestion for erroneous or non-standard uses of VPC/APC structures from Schneider and Gilquin (2016) is given in Table 3. The first column shows the verb or adjective, the second column the incorrect preposition, the third column the manually corrected preposition. *obj* means that the manual annotation suggests to use a direct object instead of a PP (e.g. *attack against someone* has manually been corrected to *attack someone*), and *n/a* means that the manually suggested correction is more complex, e.g. *diverse by* has manually been corrected to *different according to*. The ultimate column shows whether the automatic correction matches the manual correction.

5 Evaluation

We have evaluated our approach in two ways, which we describe in the following.

---

[10]We provide the full VPC and APC recommendation lists at http://pub.cl.uzh.ch/purl/reimporting_prepositions.

VERB/ADJ	PREP	CORR	MATCH?
accuse	for	of	yes
addict	on	to	yes
alarm	of	at	yes
apply	into	to	yes
assist	to	*obj*	yes
assure	to	*obj*	yes
aspire	for	to	yes
attack	against	*obj*	yes
aware	about	of	yes
belong	into	to	yes
benefit	out	from	yes
call	like	*obj*	no
characterize	with	by	yes
charge	of	with	yes
confront	to	with	yes
consist	on	of	yes
deal	about	with	yes
deprive	from	of	yes
destructive	for	to	yes
discuss	about	*obj*	yes
estimate	to	at	yes
extend	of	to	no
impose	to	on	yes
indulge	into	in	yes
interest	for	in	no
involve	into	in	yes
relate	with	to	yes
replace	to	by	no
resist	to	*obj*	yes
select	among	from	no
separate	between	*n/a*	no
study	about	*obj*	yes
understand	towards	*obj*	yes
view	upon	on	no
bad	to	for	no
capable	in	of	yes
conscious	about	of	yes
critical	against	of	yes
critical	towards	of	yes
dependent	from	on	yes
dependent	of	on	yes
diverse	by	*n/a*	no
guilty	for	of	yes
independent	on	of	yes
responsible	of	for	yes
superior	than	to	yes
synonymous	to	with	yes
worth	for	*obj*	no
Total			38/48

Table 3: Incorrect VPC/APC together with the correction suggested by our algorithm. The list of incorrect VPC/APC structures originates from (Schneider and Gilquin 2016).

First, we have evaluated the list of language-independent suggestions. In column 3 of table 2, we consider an item a true positive if it contains a non-semantic, non-compositional preposition, or if the preposition is language-specific. Precision is at 72 %. Our method does not seem to work reliably on the preposition 'into', which does not exist as a preposition in most languages, but which is semantically transparent. We thus decided to exclude this preposition in the second evaluation, given in columns 4-6, in which we check if errors corresponding to this type occur in learner corpora. 74 % of the remaining combinations are found in at least one of the learner corpora.

Second, we have tested the ability of our method to correct frequent non-standard or erroneous verb- and adjective-preposition combinations. The results are given in Table 3. PREP is the erroneous preposition, CORR the suggested correction by our algorithm, and MATCH? indicates if the suggested correction is correct. The results indicate a precision of 79.2 %, and the upper bound (*n/a* cannot be predicted correctly) is 95.8 %. Some of the errors may stem from the fact that the European parliament uses some fixed phrases that are rare in other registers.

Tetreault and Chodorow (2008) report 80 % precision at 19 % recall on the task of recognizing preposition errors in essays written by non-native students. Boyd et al. (2012) report 40 % F-score on recognizing preposition errors, and 30 % F-score on correcting them. The best performing system on the *prep* type of error in Ng, M. S. Wu, Briscoe, et al. (2014) is Felice et al. (2014), who report about 40 % precision and recall using a combination of a rule-based and an SMT approach. As their task includes both recognizing and correcting preposition errors, and all the above approaches use token-based evaluation while ours is type-based, a comparison is difficult to make, but our results appear to be competitive.

6   Conclusions

We have employed word alignment in a large parallel corpus to identify potentially difficult VPC/APC. We have compiled language-specific ranked lists in order to help learners to focus on particularly challenging combinations given their native language (L1). We have also combined the language-specific findings into a list of generally difficult combinations. As expected, Romance languages exhibit a larger overlap of combinations than German, and Polish is particularly different.

We evaluate our procedure in two ways. First we have manually assessed the precision of the language-independent list, which obtains 72 % precision. Secondly, we apply our method to an error correction task to predict the intended preposition given frequent erroneous VPC or APC. We achieved a precision of 79.2 %.

For future work, we plan to conduct the same calculations for other languages so that we will be able, for instance, to predict potentially erroneous use of German prepositions by native speakers of other languages.

Acknowledgments

This research was supported by the Swiss National Science Foundation under grant 105215_146781/1 through the project "SPARCLING – Large-scale Annotation and Alignment of Parallel Corpora for the Investigation of Linguistic Variation".

References

Aston, Guy and Lou Burnard (1998). *The BNC Handbook. Exploring the British National Corpus with SARA*. Edinburgh University Press.

Benson, Morton, Evelyn Benson, and Robert Ilson (2009). *The BBI combinatory dictionary of English: Your guide to collocations and grammar*. John Benjamins Publishing.

Boyd, Adriane, Marion Zepf, and Detmar Meurers (2012). "Informing Determiner and Preposition Error Correction with Hierarchical Word Clustering". In: *Proceedings of the 7th Workshop on Innovative Use of NLP for Building Educational Applications (BEA7)*. Montreal, Canada: Association for Computational Linguistics, pp. 208–215.

Felice, Mariano, Zheng Yuan, E. Øistein Andersen, Helen Yannakoudakis, and Ekaterina Kochmar (2014). "Grammatical error correction using hybrid systems and type filtering". In: *Proceedings of the 18th Conference on Computational Natural Language Learning (CoNLL): Shared Task*. Baltimore, Maryland: Association for Computational Linguistics, pp. 15–24.

Gao, Qin and Stephan Vogel (2008). "Parallel implementations of word alignment tool". In: *Software Engineering, Testing, and Quality Assurance for Natural Language Processing (SETQA-NLP)*. Association for Computational Linguistics, pp. 49–57.

Gardner, Dee and Mark Davies (2007). "Pointing Out Frequent Phrasal Verbs: A Corpus-Based Analysis". In: *TESOL quarterly* 41.2, pp. 339–359.

Gilquin, Gaëtanelle (2015). "The use of phrasal verbs by French-speaking EFL learners. A constructional and collostructional corpus-based approach". In: *Corpus Linguistics and Linguistic Theory* 11.1, pp. 51–88.

Gilquin, Gaëtanelle, Sylviane Granger, et al. (2011). "From EFL to ESL: evidence from the International Corpus of Learner English". In: *Exploring second-language varieties of English and learner Englishes: Bridging a paradigm gap*, pp. 55–78.

Graën, Johannes, Dolores Batinic, and Martin Volk (2014). "Cleaning the Europarl Corpus for Linguistic Applications". In: *Proceedings of the Conference on Natural Language Processing (KONVENS)*. (Hildesheim). Stiftung Universität Hildesheim, pp. 222–227.

Granger, Sylviane, Estelle Dagneaux, Fanny Meunier, and Magali Paquot (2002). *International corpus of learner English*. Presses universitaires de Louvain.

Granger, Sylviane and Marie-Aude Lefer (2016). "From general to learners' bilingual dictionaries: Towards a more effective fulfilment of advanced learners' phraseological needs". In: *International Journal of Lexicography*, pp. 279–295.

Koehn, Philipp (2005). "Europarl: A parallel corpus for statistical machine translation". In: *Machine Translation Summit*. (Phuket). Vol. 5. Asia-Pacific Association for Machine Translation (AAMT), pp. 79–86.

Liang, Percy, Ben Taskar, and Dan Klein (2006). "Alignment by agreement". In: *Proceedings of the main conference on Human Language Technology Conference of the North American Chapter of the Association of Computational Linguistics (HLT-NAACL)*, pp. 104–111.

Ng, Tou Hwee, Mei Siew Wu, Ted Briscoe, Christian Hadiwinoto, Hendy Raymond Susanto, and Christopher Bryant (2014). "The CoNLL-2014 Shared Task on Grammatical Error Correction". In: *Proceedings of the 18th Conference on Computational Natural Language Learning (CoNLL): Shared Task*. Baltimore, Maryland: Association for Computational Linguistics, pp. 1–14.

Ng, Tou Hwee, Mei Siew Wu, Yuanbin Wu, Christian Hadiwinoto, and Joel Tetreault (2013). "The CoNLL-2013 Shared Task on Grammatical Error Correction". In: *Proceedings of the 17th Conference on Computational Natural Language Learning (CoNLL): Shared Task*. Sofia: Association for Computational Linguistics, pp. 1–12.

Nivre, Joakim, Johan Hall, and Jens Nilsson (2006). "Maltparser: A data-driven parser-generator for dependency parsing". In: *Proceedings of the 5th International Conference on Language Resources and Evaluation (LREC)*. Vol. 6, pp. 2216–2219.

Och, Franz Josef and Hermann Ney (2003). "A Systematic Comparison of Various Statistical Alignment Models". In: *Computational linguistics* 29.1, pp. 19–51.

Petrov, Slav, Dipanjan Das, and Ryan McDonald (2012). "A Universal Part-of-Speech Tagset". In: *Proceedings of the 8th International Conference on Language Resources and Evaluation (LREC)*.

Schmid, Helmut (1994). "Probabilistic part-of-speech tagging using decision trees". In: *Proceedings of International Conference on New Methods in Natural Language Processing (NeMLaP)*. (Manchester). Vol. 12, pp. 44–49.

Schneider, Gerold and Gaëtanelle Gilquin (2016). "Detecting Innovations in a Parsed Corpus of Learner English". In: *International Journal of Learner Corpus Research* 2.2.

Tetreault, R. Joel and Martin Chodorow (2008). "The Ups and Downs of Preposition Error Detection in ESL Writing". In: *Proceedings of the 22nd International Conference on Computational Linguistics (COLING)*. Manchester: COLING 2008 Organizing Committee, pp. 865–872.

Varga, Dániel, Péter Halácsy, András Kornai, Viktor Nagy, László Németh, and Viktor Trón (2005). "Parallel corpora for medium density languages". In: *Proceedings of the Recent Advances in Natural Language Processing (RANLP)*. (Borovets), pp. 590–596.

Volk, Martin, Chantal Amrhein, Noëmi Aepli, Mathias Müller, and Phillip Ströbel (2016). "Building a Parallel Corpus on the World's Oldest Banking Magazine". In: *Proceedings of the Conference on Natural Language Processing (KONVENS)*. (Bochum).

Yannakoudakis, Helen, Ted Briscoe, and Ben Medlock (2011). "A new dataset and method for automatically grading ESOL texts". In: *Proceedings of the 49th Annual Meeting of the Association for Computational Linguistics: Human Language Technologies (ACL-HLT)*. Vol. 1, pp. 180–189.

A   Most relevant VPC for English learners with L1 being German and French

| | German | | | | | French | | | |
no	λ_v	λ_p	$\lambda_{p''}$	BTR		λ_v	λ_p	$\lambda_{p''}$	BTR
1	think	of	on	1.09		deal	with	of	2.07
2	impose	on	for	1.36		provide	for	of	1.24
3	hope	for	on	1.07		call	for	of	1.82
4	remind	of	on	1.22		decide	on	of	1.05
5	prevent	from	of	1.83		comply	with	of	1.60
6	consist	of	from	1.38		hope	for	of	1.00
7	postpone	until	by	1.06		ask	for	of	2.08
8	exclude	from	of	1.64		face	with	in	1.65
9	aim	at	on	2.74		push	for	of	1.07
10	talk	about	on	3.34		confront	with	in	1.19
11	look	at	in	3.40		cope	with	in	1.47
12	gain	from	of	1.42		reserve	for	in	1.19
13	deliver	on	in	1.37		inflict	on	in	1.11
14	receive	from	of	2.00		spend	on	for	1.75
15	emanate	from	of	1.19		apologise	for	of	1.26
16	compose	of	from	1.30		qualify	for	of	1.15
17	wait	for	on	2.25		strive	for	of	1.32
18	embark	on	in	1.69		associate	with	in	1.92
19	compliment	on	for	1.49		wait	for	of	1.99
20	benefit	from	of	2.72		aim	at	in	2.81
21	shed	on	in	1.62		last	for	of	1.23
22	suffer	from	under	2.44		expire	on	in	1.25
23	dispense	with	on	1.57		allow	for	of	2.28
24	stop	from	of	1.88		arrange	for	of	1.44
25	warn	against	before	1.82		cater	for	of	1.45
26	protect	from	before	2.42		confer	on	in	1.79
27	test	on	in	1.65		look	at	in	5.08
28	abstain	from	in	2.42		account	for	of	2.50
29	hear	from	of	2.65		arrive	at	in	2.77
30	refrain	from	of	2.44		embark	on	in	2.37
31	inform	of	on	2.92		blame	for	of	2.28
32	profit	from	of	2.14		direct	at	in	2.79
33	free	from	of	2.21		destine	for	in	2.27
34	direct	at	on	2.74		estimate	at	in	2.42
35	spend	on	for	3.76		resume	at	in	2.31
36	target	at	on	2.66		burden	with	of	2.28
37	worry	about	on	3.01		concern	with	of	4.26
38	estimate	at	on	2.49		align	with	on	2.59
39	recover	from	of	2.45		fill	with	of	2.69
40	delight	with	on	2.65		congratulate	on	for	6.68
41	depend	on	of	5.01		depend	on	of	5.77
42	arrive	at	in	4.07		search	for	of	2.98
43	exempt	from	of	3.13		level	at	in	3.04
44	differ	from	of	3.62		please	with	of	4.43
45	level	at	on	2.99		care	for	of	3.59
46	depart	from	of	3.24		dispense	with	of	3.34
47	expect	from	of	3.91		forgive	for	of	4.25
48	complain	about	on	3.55		target	at	on	4.74

B   Most relevant VPC for English learners with L1 being Spanish and Polish

| | Spanish | | | | | Polish | | | |
no	λ_v	λ_p	$\lambda_{p''}$	BTR		λ_v	λ_p	$\lambda_{p''}$	BTR
1	thank	for	by	1.01		talk	about	of	1.40
2	deal	with	of	1.36		vote	in	for	2.16
3	call	for	of	1.16		ask	for	of	1.61
4	ask	for	of	1.15		allow	for	on	1.17
5	impose	on	in	1.10		look	at	on	2.29
6	consist	of	in	1.02		deprive	of	by	1.00
7	pass	on	of	1.08		concern	with	of	1.37
8	build	on	in	1.09		wait	for	on	1.47
9	hope	for	of	1.17		hope	for	on	1.24
10	allow	for	of	1.31		learn	from	with	1.48
11	wait	for	of	1.50		remove	from	with	1.33
12	equip	with	of	1.01		pass	on	in	1.48
13	apologise	for	by	1.04		press	for	on	1.14
14	compensate	for	of	1.19		schedule	for	on	1.10
15	think	of	in	1.85		aim	at	on	2.37
16	concern	with	of	1.66		confer	on	in	1.13
17	argue	for	of	1.15		fight	for	of	1.62
18	aim	at	in	2.45		regard	as	for	2.02
19	base	on	in	3.66		compose	of	with	1.10
20	congratulate	on	by	2.53		discriminate	against	of	1.34
21	deliver	on	in	1.21		decide	on	of	1.93
22	qualify	for	of	1.11		depend	on	from	2.17
23	pick	on	of	1.12		avail	of	with	1.09
24	punish	for	by	1.02		fill	with	by	1.16
25	touch	on	in	1.62		benefit	from	with	2.24
26	arrange	for	of	1.24		worry	about	of	1.50
27	elaborate	on	in	1.22		label	of	in	1.22
28	acquaint	with	of	1.32		escape	from	with	1.20
29	destine	for	of	1.48		congratulate	on	in	3.03
30	inflict	on	in	1.55		withdraw	from	with	1.52
31	focus	on	in	4.01		burden	with	of	1.16
32	place	on	in	3.05		dispose	of	in	1.35
33	confer	on	in	1.89		suffer	from	of	2.04
34	cater	for	of	1.77		exclude	from	with	1.98
35	impact	on	in	1.94		emerge	from	with	2.03
36	direct	at	in	2.37		derive	from	with	1.98
37	account	for	of	2.81		originate	from	with	1.64
38	search	for	of	2.04		gain	from	with	1.83
39	rest	on	in	2.17		arise	from	with	2.26
40	arrive	at	in	3.18		exempt	from	with	1.70
41	resume	at	in	2.16		report	on	of	2.12
42	look	at	in	6.99		protect	from	before	2.22
43	dwell	on	in	2.51		recover	from	with	1.64
44	spend	on	in	3.78		release	from	with	1.69
45	concentrate	on	in	4.41		stem	from	with	2.11
46	insist	on	in	4.31		touch	on	in	2.33
47	rely	on	in	4.00		import	from	with	2.13
48	compliment	on	by	2.70		quote	from	with	1.91

Revita: a System for Language Learning and Supporting Endangered Languages

Anisia Katinskaia, Javad Nouri, Roman Yangarber
University of Helsinki
Department of Computer Science
`first.last@cs.helsinki.fi`

Abstract

We describe a computational system for language learning and supporting endangered languages. The platform provides the user an opportunity to improve her competency through *active* language use. The platform currently works with several endangered Finno-Ugric languages, as well as with Yakut, and Finnish, Swedish, and Russian. This paper describes the current stage of ongoing development.

1 Introduction

Revita is an open online platform designed to help support endangered languages, by stimulating *active* language learning. Current focus is on several endangered languages inside the Russian Federation (RF), which have moderate to small numbers of speakers, including several Finno-Ugric (F-U) languages—Udmurt, Meadow Mari, Erzya, Komi-Zyrian, North Saami—and Sakha (Yakut), a Turkic language.[1] The system also works with Finnish, Swedish, and Russian, for several practical reasons. Finnish is structurally very similar to many Uralic languages. Further, texts in many of the target languages often exhibit spontaneous code-switching into Russian, so a Russian component has emerged as an essential feature of the system.

The tool is aimed at people who already possess some competence in the target language—intermediate to advanced students (i.e., not for the very beginners).

The rest of the paper is organized as follows: Section 2 is devoted to a review of prior work in the area of generating "cloze" exercises, Section 3 describes exercise generation in the Revita system and related research problems, and Section 4 presents the conclusions.

2 Prior work

Computer-aided language learning (CALL) was first introduced in the 1950s, and since then has developed significantly as technology evolved. We briefly mention some relevant systems, such as PLATO, (Hart, 1981), and (Chapelle and Jamieson, 1983), which was one of the first and most significant systems for teaching and learning languages. Macario was one of the first video programs for learning Spanish (Gale, 1989); the Athena Language-Learning Project (ALLP) combined "interactivity and more primitive drill-and-practice routine" (Murray, 2014); programs like *À la rencontre de Phillippe* (Murray, 2014) allowed learners to act in the learning language environment. Thousands of other programs have been created. Some of the programs, such as Robo-Sensei (Nagata, 2002) and E-Tutor (Heift, 2001), use NLP (natural language processing) techniques, and may be called "intelligent" CALL systems.

Revita's main learning mode involves a type of exercise known as "*cloze*" in the literature, first described in (Taylor, 1953). In a cloze (deletion) test, a portion of text has some of the words removed, and the learner is asked to recover the missing words. Clozes require an understanding of the context, semantics and syntax in order to identify the missing words correctly.

The approach in (Zesch and Melamud, 2014) involves generating *distractors* for vocabulary clozes—multiple-choice questions. The method for generating lists of distractors is as follows. First "context-insensitive inference rules" are used to generate a set of candidate distractors. This set includes the top-N matches for the target word w in the corpus—words which share some con-

---

[1] All F-U languages are inside RF, except Finnish, Hungarian, North Saami, and Estonian.

Anisia Katinskaia, Javad Nouri and Roman Yangarber 2017. Revita: a system for language learning and supporting endangered languages. *Proceedings of the Joint 6th Workshop on NLP for Computer Assisted Language Learning and 2nd Workshop on NLP for Research on Language Acquisition at NoDaLiDa 2017.* Linköping Electronic Conference Proceedings 134: 27–35.

text words with w, which harvests words that are in some sense similar. Then the top-M matches are found which appear in exactly the same context as the cloze item ("context-sensitive inference rules"). A distractor blacklist specifies words that should not be used as distractors. In case there are a large number of distractors, ranking is applied to select the most challenging ones. These can be the less frequent distractors in the corpus, or the most similar to the target word (provided that they are not in the blacklist).

Smith et al. (2010) presented an approach to generation of vocabulary clozes, for English only. Their system takes a key (the target word), chooses distractors from a distributional thesaurus, and identifies a collocate that does not occur with the distractors using "Sketch Engine," a corpus query system. Then the system finds a sentence containing the pair. The best sentence should not be long, with sufficient useful context.

Lee and Seneff (2007) describe an approach to generating distractors for learning English prepositions. Distractors are defined in terms of *usability*—only one choice is correct, requiring minimum post-editing time—and in terms of *difficulty* which means that distractors are on the right level of difficulty, neither too wrong nor too challenging, making these choices appropriate for the less proficient language users.

Pino et al. (2008) present a strategy for improving automatically generated cloze and open-cloze (without multiple choice) questions, used by the REAP tutoring system for English as a Second Language vocabulary learning. The system provides the learner with documents retrieved from the Web, filtered for quality and annotated for topic and readability level, to match the student's interest and the model of the student's vocabulary knowledge. For selecting sentences with target words, the system scores sentence complexity, measured by counting the number of clauses, as identified by the Stanford parser. The context of sentences with more clauses is believed to be more well-defined. However, in essence, how well-defined the context is depends on the possibility of replacing the target word with any other word. This can be measured by sum the collocation scores between the target word and other words in the sentence. The authors provide an example: the sentence "I drank a cup of strong (blank) with lemon and sugar" is very well-defined for "tea" because of high collocation scores between "tea" and "strong," "lemon", "sugar", "drink." In absence of these strong collocations, it is less likely to define a target word from the context. This approach showed better results than a baseline.

One of the main problems with this approach is that distractors may fit the context semantically, so open cloze questions can have more than one plausible answer. Also, sentence selection is problematic, since a single sentence may not provide sufficient information for choosing the correct answer.

Brown et al. (2005) present six types of questions for evaluating the level of vocabulary knowledge of REAP system users. This evaluation is used to update the user model of vocabulary knowledge, to provide new texts with 95% of words familiar to the user and 5% of new words. Using WordNet data, the following types of questions were generated: choosing the definition of a word, selecting synonyms and antonyms, hypernym and hyponym question types (completing phrases), and cloze questions. It is shown that there is a correlation between computer-generated questions for assessment of vocabulary skills and human-written questions.

Chen et al. (2006) describe the principles for generation of tests on grammaticality for English language. Tests are based on manually-designed patterns, e.g., the pattern {VB VBG} means that some verb requires a gerund as a complement ("My friends enjoy traveling by plane"). Distractors are usually constructed based on words in the pattern with some modifications, such as changing some grammatical meaning, part of speech, reordering words. Gathered from the Web, sentences are transformed into tests based on the patterns. There are two types of tests: multiple choice and error detection. All tests were evaluated by experts and 77-80% were regarded as "worthy".

Shei (2001) presents the concept *FollowYou!*, which transforms a raw text into language lessons, giving the student an opportunity to read his/her favourite articles with textbook-support. The learner's vocabulary knowledge is tested and recorded in the Profile Manager, which decides which words should be included in the next lesson. The Lesson Generator extracts definitions of the chosen words from the Dictionary, the collocations, their synonyms, and example sentences from the corpus. To test the effectiveness of the

Figure 1: Story practice mode: exercises presented randomly from text.

lesson and to update the user's vocabulary model, some exercises need to be solved, e.g., gap-filling exercises. The main idea behind that project is that authentic materials—created by and for native speakers—are essential for the language learner.

3 Main principles and features

The main principle of our project is stimulating active language use in the process of learning from a text. By this we mean *active production* of required language forms while reading texts, rather than passive absorption of language examples or rules. We focus on learning the grammar as well as the vocabulary. Exercises provided by the system—including multiple-choice quizzes for indeclinable parts of speech, crosswords automatically generated from stories, can be regarded as grammar and vocabulary practice because the learner needs to produce words in context. Flashcards are available for vocabulary learning.

The platform has a small library of stories for each language. However, the main idea is that students will upload a variety of texts from web pages or plain text files to their personal library. Personal libraries can be shared between users. Studying language by reading stories, in which the students are interested implies personal involvement in learning process, it reduces boredom factor, and increases motivation to use the online plat-form. Moreover, texts uploaded from the Internet and mostly intended for native speakers will catalyze cultural enrichment and immersion into the specifics of language use and conventions.

One important system feature is that adding a new language is a simple procedure if a morphological analyzer is available for the language of interest. However, without language-specific adjustments and sets of rules, based on which the more complex exercises can be created, the kinds of available exercises will be limited and the range of grammatical concepts, which can be practiced, will also be restricted.

Exercises are created from any story automatically by analyzing words in the text and deciding on the best words to practice. The choice of words is based on the student's answers given so far, which the program remembers and assesses automatically. Tracking the students progress is one of the key features which we plan to develop during further research.

3.1 Essential exercise modes

There are two essential exercise modes provided by the system at present: the "practice" mode and the crossword mode. In the *practice mode*, see Figure 1, the learner chooses a story which s/he wants to practice and then receives pieces of this story in order. Each piece (called a "snippet")

Figure 2: Crossword generated from Sakha story

includes approximately 30-40 words, respecting sentence boundaries. Several words in the snippet will be chosen for quizzes, as the result of a randomized selection process. For each quiz word, the learner receives a gap in the text, and one of two types of quizzes: a multiple-choice quiz, where the learner must select one word from a list. Multiple-choice quiz is can be generated for non-inflected words, like prepositions, postpositions, adverbs, etc. The second type of quiz—cloze quiz—is used for inflected parts of speech: nouns, verbs, adjectives. The base form (lemma) is shown, and the learner needs to guess the correct grammatical surface form in the context. For example: "Topelius kertoo Maamme kirja eri maakunnista" ("Topelius tells book Our Land about the different provinces."). The word in the box is a lemma which is presented as a hint to the user. The task is to derive the surface form from this lemma in the given context. The correct inflected surface form in this example is "kirjassaan" ("in his book").

After producing with all quiz words in the current snippet, the learner receives immediate feedback about his/her answers, and the next snippet for practice. The student receives points for correct answers, and points are removed if the user makes mistakes. It is important to stress that the correct form means the same as the form found in the story. This approach to assessment is convenient because we only rely on that the author chose to include in the story. However, it also has drawbacks because the user may insert a form which is allowed by the context but is not the same as the form used by the author in the story. This problem is one of the topics for further research.

Crosswords are generated from the story (or from a part of the story) automatically and consist of 40–50 words, see Figure 2. Users receive the story as an exercise, with some of the words removed, and a crossword based on the missing words. The task is to guess the words in their correct grammatical form. If the forms inserted by the user are correct, they will be added to the story and highlighted in green. Since this task can be difficult even for a native speaker, the user can request an additional hint for any missing word, which is its grammatical base form (lemma). The student

Proceedings of the Joint 6th Workshop on NLP for Computer Assisted Language Learning and 2nd Workshop on NLP for Research on Language Acquisition at NoDaLiDa 2017

30

receives points for solving the words.

During work on the current snippet, the student can request a translation of any word (more precisely, of its lemmas) in the snippet. The translation is shown in the box on the left, Figure 1. It is important to clarify the notion of *ambiguous* words in Revita. A word-form is considered as ambiguous if it has more than one different lemma. For instance, words with different, unrelated meanings can have homonymous forms but different base forms. For example, the Russian surface forms "жил" has two morphological bases: "жить" (live-INF, *"to live"*) and "жила" (sinew-NOM.SG, *"sinew"*). In the first case, "жил" is the past tense, masculine gender form of the verb (live-PST.MASC.SG, *"he lived"*), in the second case "жил" is the genitive plural form of the noun, (sinew-GEN.PL, *"sinew"*). If a word-form in the story is ambiguous, the system tries to provide translations of all base forms.

For Finnish, Swedish, and Russian, Revita uses the Glosbe multi-language dictionary[2] with a possibility to translate into a number of languages. FU-Lab dictionaries[3] are used to translate from Komi-Zyrian, Meadow Mari, and Udmurt into Russian. Revita uses *sakhatyla.ru* for translating from Sakha into Russian and English. The default destination language for translation will be the same as the language chosen by the user as the language of the interface (currently English, Finnish, Swedish or Russian) if dictionaries for these languages are available. For instance, for Komi-Zyrian, Udmurt, and Meadow Mari, translation is available only into Russian at the present stage. All words that the student has clicked on to get translations are automatically saved to the personal dictionary. Words the dictionary are used for practice as *flashcards*, with the lemma on one side of the card and its translations on the other side.

3.2 Generating exercises

Any uploaded text is first tokenised, the title is identified and the text is analysed by a morphological analyser. Revita uses the following tools:

- morphological analysers for Uralic languages, from GiellaTekno[4];
- the Crosslator Tagger (Klyshinsky et al., 2011) morphological analyzer for Russian;

- the HFST toolkit[5] for analyzing Swedish;
- *sakhatyla.ru*,[6] morphological analyser of online Sakha-Russian-Sakha translator system.

We extract base forms, parts of speech, and grammatical tags from the morphological analyses. Split into words and analysed, stories are saved into the database.

After morphological analysis, the system extracts from the text all words and combinations of words which can serve as candidates for practice. Every candidate is assigned to a particular snippet of the story and saved in the database. To be chosen as candidates, singleton words should have the same base form for all analyses returned by the analyser, otherwise, a word cannot be used for practice because the system cannot decide what base have to be offered as a hint. Combinations of words are chosen by the system based on language-specific rules; all words in a combination are considered to be disambiguated.

Choosing only unambiguous singleton words as candidates is a problem for the system because it limits the range of words and grammatical concepts which can be presented in exercises. For example, Udmurt forms in reflexive voice are homonymous to present tense forms, e.g., the verb "дасяны" (prepare-INF, *"to prepare"*) has a form "дасясько" (prepare-PRES.3.SG, *"s/he prepares"*) with the meaning of singular present tense, and another verb "дасяськыны" (prerare-INF-REFL, *"to prepare oneself"*) has the homonymous form "дасясько" (prepare-PRES-REFL.3.SG, *"s/he prepares her/himself"*), where the latter form has the meaning of reflexive voice. It means that the form "дасясько" is ambiguous (has two different lemmas) and will never be chosen as a candidate by Revita. Consequently, the reflexive voice cannot currently be practiced for Udmurt for words with the same paradigm.

Combinations of words are chosen by Revita based on language-specific rules. For instance, the system contains rules for Russian, such as:

1. [pos=adj, case=X, number=Y, gender=Z] [pos=noun, case=X, number=Y, gender=Z];

2. [word=в, pos=prep] [case=loc or acc].

The rules make reference to the word's parts of speech and morphological tags. The first

---

[2]https://glosbe.com
[3]http://dict.fu-lab.ru
[4]http://giellatekno.uit.no

[5]https://kitwiki.csc.fi

[6]*Sakhatyla.ru* is created by Vasiliy Ivanov and has a web-interface available here[7] and a Telegram messenger application bot.

rule defines agreement between a noun-adjective pair. The second rule defines prepositional government—which cases are governed by the specific preposition, в ("in"). These rules drive the selection of sequences of words from the story, such as "красивой девушке", "в доме", which correspond to the specified rules as follows:

"красивой девушке"

   beautiful-Fem.Dat.Sg girl-Fem.Dat.Sg

    "... [to] a beautiful girl (dative)"

"в доме"

   in house-Loc.Sg

    "In a/the house"

Any possible ambiguity in the sequences matched by the rules is expected to be resolved[8] by virtue of the context. Sequences selected (randomly) by these rules will be offered as quizzes for practice as cloze-type exercises—the learner again receives as a hint only the lemmas of these words—or as multiple-choice quizzes. In case the sequence includes indeclinable words (such as a preposition, in the second rule, above) other prepositions with similar meaning will be used as distractors. Depending on the learner's results on other tasks, the system will offer exercises of various levels of complexity. For example, for sequences matching the above rules, we may produce:

- multiple-choice quiz for a preposition, all other surface forms given;
- one inflected surface form as cloze quiz (only the lemma given);
- one inflected word is as cloze quiz, multiple-choice quiz for a preposition;
- both noun and adjective surface forms as (coordinated) cloze quizzes, and multiple-choice for a preposition.

All of the learner's answers are stored in the database, both correct and incorrect. The entire history of the learner's answers is used for selecting exercises in subsequent snippets. Revita uses the history to compute weights for exercise candidates—non-ambiguous singleton words, and sequences of words that match rules. Examples which never always answered correctly by the learner receive a low probability (so they are not chosen frequently, to avoid boring the learner). Examples which were answered some-

---

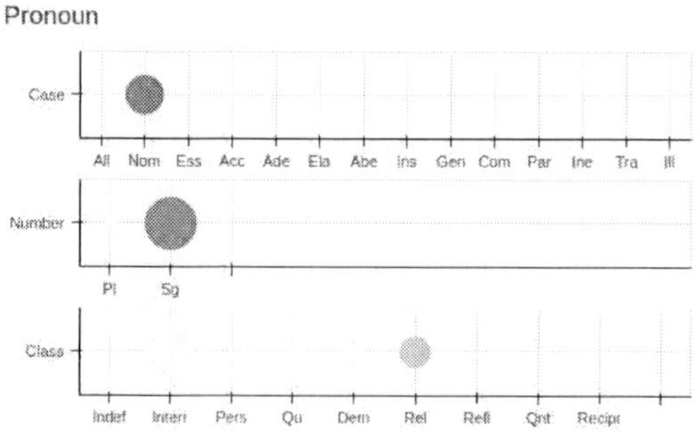

Figure 3: Progress visualisation for Finnish pronouns

times correctly and sometimes incorrectly receive high probability. Examples that were never answered correctly receive a lower weight again. Any time when the user starts practicing a new snippet, a probability of next candidates for practice is calculated. The system also controls the spread and proximity of the candidates within the snippet—they should not be too close to each other to provide sufficient context for each exercise. This randomness is applied when choosing from the set of all candidates—this allows each story to be practiced *multiple times*, with new exercises being chosen on each round. When the learner starts over, the system will select a new set of words for practice, which may partially overlap with the set of words chosen on the previous round.

At the current stage, the system provides an initial version of the learner's progress assessment. Revita checks all answers which the learner has provided during the exercises, and identifies which grammatical concepts were answered correctly what proportion of time; the concepts include grammatical categories, such as case, number, tense, etc. The learner (or teacher) can track progress via a visualisation page, which displays how the user performed on various concepts, see Figure 3. The more a grammatical concepts has been exercised the bigger its circle; the color ranges from green for mostly correct answers to red for mostly incorrect ones.

3.3 Code-switching disambiguation

Choosing words for exercises needs some care for certain languages, where a special kind of ambiguity arises. For example, texts in many of the F-U languages often include instances of *code-switching* into Russian. Code-switching is a normal and common phenomenon; however, only

---

[8]It is possible to construct (somewhat artificial) examples, where ambiguous words match these syntactic patterns and yet do not form the expected construction. If needed, this problem can be alleviated by various NLP techniques—by taking *wider* context into account.

words from the target language[9] should be chosen for practice. The problem arises when a Komi text has a surface form, X, which is a code-switch into Russian, and yet X happens to be **also** a valid word-form in Komi (with an unrelated meaning).[10] For example, X may be the surface form "пота". In Komi it is first-person singular indicative of the verb "потны" ("to crack"). The same word-form also happens to be the genitive of Russian "пот" ("sweat"). If we ignore the Russian, and X happens to be an instance of a code-switch (a Russian phrase inserted into the Komi text), then Revita will provide the Komi verb stem "потны" as a "hint."

In general, the clear danger is that Revita may incorrectly treat X as a Komi word-form, extract its Komi lemma and inappropriately offer the lemma as a "hint" to the learner in a cloze quiz—this would be terribly misleading, causing the system to lose credibility with the user.

To prevent this type of mistake, several methods may be applied. We present a simple solution, which works well for the present.[11] We apply morphological analysers for both Komi and Russian to *all* words in Komi text. If a word has only a Komi analysis, it becomes a candidate for exercises. If it has only a Russian analysis, it is definitely excluded as Russian. The last case is when the word has both analyses. We don't want to simply remove all such words from the list of candidates for exercises.[12] Thus, we apply this algorithm to identify and discard *"risky"* Russian words:

- for all words w with both Russian and Komi analyses;
- we look through the entire text and check whether w has *"friends,"* i.e., whether its base form is equal to the base form of some *other* surface form y in the story. We check this property, because we expect Komi words to repeat in the story. All words without friends are discarded as risky—they are potential Russian words mistaken as Komi. If

w has Komi friends in the story, it is highly likely to be a true Komi word.

- If w has friends, we examine its *"neighbors."* The word is again discarded as risky if it has at least one direct neighbor with a Russian analysis, because we expect that Russian words are more likely to appear as part of entire phrases than as isolated words.

To evaluate the accuracy of the algorithm, we took a sample of 5% of all words having both a Russian and an Udmurt analysis and computed the accuracy of the prediction made by the algorithm:

$$accuracy = \frac{TP + TN}{all}$$

where TP are true positives—words marked as Udmurt by the algorithm, which an expert confirmed to be Udmurt. TN are true negatives—non-Udmurt words which the algorithm marked as Russian. We manually checked the sample of words with Russian and Udmurt analyses in our corpus of stories. The obtained accuracy was 0.77. We should note that Crosslator Tagger sometimes returns a Russian analysis for non-Russian words, which increases the number of false positives (words which are not really risky), and brings down the accuracy measure.[13]

Because we expect the learner to produce the grammatical form which is equal to the form found in the story, we assume that there is only one correct answer in a particular context. However, we can have lexical and grammatical synonyms which suit the same context, as well as *optional* grammatical meanings which may or may not be expressed in this context, which may make it difficult for the user to guess the correct grammatical form only from the lemma. The system should not choose such cases for practice or should be more intelligent and tolerate optional or grammatically equivalent markers. For instance, in Komi-Zyrian the same grammatical meaning can have different forms, e.g., verb "лоны" (*"to be"*) in the indicative mood, first past tense, third person singular has two valid forms with the same meaning in the same context — "лои" and "лоис". Thus, the learner cannot decide which form is expected by the system. Solving that problem is non-trivial because it requires sufficient amounts of data to build a reliable language model. We plan to start with

---

[9]In this section we will refer Komi as a "representative," to avoid writing repetitively *"a F-U language that uses the Cyrillic alphabet and therefore may contain word-forms confusable with Russian."*

[10]Note, this does not apply to *borrowings*, where Russian words are borrowed into Komi, and inflected according to Komi morphological rules.

[11]More robust and ultimately better solutions will involve building statistical language models, planned for future work.

[12]In Udmurt, e.g., they represent 19% of all words in our corpus.

[13]We have tested only Udmurt, we will test with other languages which exhibit code-switching into Russian.

Finnish and Russian because for other languages data is more difficult to obtain.

4 Conclusions and future plans

The Revita system is under development, therefore there are many outstanding problems to be solved and improvements to be added. Continuing the above discussion, presenting an appropriate hint to the learner is crucial, because misleading hints (lemmas for cloze quizzes and distractors for multiple-choice quizzes) will cause the learner frustration and will discourage the continued use of the system. Further, we must solve many language-specific problems. While for some languages, like Russian or Finnish, it may be done by building language models, for languages like Erzya, Komi-Zyrian, or Sakha we may have to develop rule-based solutions, due to a lack of corpora. Also, many difficulties are caused by erroneous analyses. We discussed the process of generating exercises at the current stage and related problems. Further kinds of exercises can be developed for different languages depending on the available language resources.

The system was tested by several users, and we plan to collect more formal results about its efficacy.

Revita offers several types of exercises generated from any story. The systems assesses the answers given by user by comparing them with forms found in the story and it cannot accept other answers which are allowed in the context.

Users can translate any word in the story and to save them as flashcards. Based on the flashcards, Revita provides vocabulary exercises. Vocabulary learning in general and vocabulary learning with help of computers was studied, e.g., by (Nation, 2013), (Ahmed, 1989), (Laufer and Hill, 2000), (Prince, 1996). Learning new words in context is more preferable than learning words in isolation— see (Groot, 2000) and (Krashen, 1989)—to better understand their semantic and syntactic features. This is consistent with one the main principles of the system, namely, learning language while reading. The learner does not only infer the meaning of a new word from the context, but also can link it with a translation into the learner's native language. Efficiency of such linking is questioned, despite the efficiency in terms of quantity, see (Prince, 1996). Nevertheless, we assume this linking to be beneficial provided that there are other approaches to learning offered in parallel. This may involve establishing links between a new word and other words in the language, e.g., through exercises with synonyms, where the learner should decide which word among a list of synonyms is the most appropriate in the context, and to generate the correct grammatical form of the chosen word. This type of exercise can also include practicing of multi-word expressions.

Further aspects which we plan to develop are:

- refining the scoring system which should not "only lead to a learner's pursuit of meaningless 'points' with little or no regard for learning" (Beatty, 2013) but works to stimulate the user to learn more;

- adding the possibility for collaboration to the system, since some of the pedagogical objectives can be achieved better through group activity—solving problems in a group, discussing them with experts/teachers also registered in the system.

- assessment of uploaded stories by their difficulty for the learner, and their quality as learning material. This is important because the learner decides which stories to practice, and the system should help guide learners in some may.

- progress detection which is important for developing new exercises and their assessment.

Progress detection and assessment involves comparing previous responses of the user and identifying the development of his/her knowledge, targeting weak areas, and generating exercises for the next stage, depending on all this information, and returning intelligent and useful feedback to the learner.[14] Development of this functionality is one of the main future steps in the Revita system.

Acknowledgments

This work was supported by the FinUgRevita Project of the Academy of Finland. We thank Larisa Ponomareva for help with the Permic languages, Sardana Ivanova for help with Sakha, Max Koppatz and Kim Salmi for their contributions to the software development.

---

[14]This is a challenge, since we wish to avoid assuming that the learner is familiar with any linguistic or grammatical concepts; the system should serve non-specialists equally well.

References

Medani Osman Ahmed. 1989. Vocabulary learning strategies. *Beyond words*, pages 3–14.

Ken Beatty. 2013. *Teaching & researching: Computer-assisted language learning*. Routledge.

J. Brown, G. Firshkoff, and M. Eskenazi. 2005. Automatic question generation for vocabulary assessment. In *Proceedings of HLT/EMNLP-2005*.

Carol Chapelle and Joan Jamieson. 1983. Language lessons on the PLATO IV system. *System*, 11(1):13–20.

C. Chen, H. Liou, and J. Chang. 2006. Fast—an automatic generation system for grammar tests. In *Proceedings of the COLING/ACL, Interactive Presentation Sessions*.

Larrie E Gale. 1989. Macario, Montevidisco, and interactive Dígame: Developing interactive video for language instruction. *Modern technology in foreign language education: Applications and projects*, pages 235–247.

Peter JM Groot. 2000. Computer assisted second language vocabulary acquisition. *Language Learning & Technology*, 4(1):60–81.

Robert Hart. 1981. Language study and the PLATO system. *Studies in Language Learning*, 3(1):1–24.

Trude Heift. 2001. Intelligent language tutoring systems for grammar practice. *Zeitschrift für Interkulturellen Fremdsprachenunterricht*, 6(2).

ES Klyshinsky, NA Kochetkova, MI Litvinov, and V Yu Maximov. 2011. Method of POS-disambiguation using information about words co-occurrence (for Russian). *Proc. of GSCL*, pages 191–195.

Stephen Krashen. 1989. We acquire vocabulary and spelling by reading: Additional evidence for the input hypothesis. *The modern language journal*, 73(4):440–464.

Batia Laufer and Monica Hill. 2000. What lexical information do L2 learners select in a CALL dictionary and how does it affect word retention? *Language Learning & Technology*, 3(2):58–76.

John Lee and Stephanie Seneff. 2007. Automatic generation of cloze items for prepositions. In *Proceedings of INTERSPEECH*, Antwerp, Belgium.

Denise E Murray. 2014. *Knowledge machines: Language and information in a technological society*. Routledge.

Noriko Nagata. 2002. Banzai: An application of natural language processing to web-based language learning. *CALICO journal*, pages 583–599.

Ian Stephen Paul Nation. 2013. *Teaching & learning vocabulary*. Boston: Heinle Cengage Learning.

Juan Pino, Michael Heilman, and Maxine Eskenazi. 2008. A selection strategy to improve cloze question quality. In *Proceedings of the Workshop on Intelligent Tutoring Systems for Ill-Defined Domains at the 9th Internationnal Conference on Intelligent Tutoring Systems*.

Peter Prince. 1996. Second language vocabulary learning: The role of context versus translations as a function of proficiency. *The modern language journal*, 80(4):478–493.

Chi-Chiang Shei. 2001. FollowYou!: An automatic language lesson generation system. *Computer Assisted Language Learning*, 14(2).

Simon Smith, P V S Avinesh, and Adam Kilgarriff. 2010. Gap-fill tests for language learners: Corpus-driven item generation. In *Proceedings of ICON-2010: 8th International Conference on Natural Language Processing*.

W. L. Taylor. 1953. Cloze procedure: A new tool for measuring readability. *Journalism Quarterly*, 30.

Torsten Zesch and Oren Melamud. 2014. Automatic generation of challenging distractors using context-sensitive inference rules. In *Proceedings of the Ninth Workshop on Innovative Use of NLP for Building Educational Applications*, pages 143–148, Baltimore, Maryland, USA.

Developing A Web-based Workbook for English Supporting the Interaction of Students and Teachers

Björn Rudzewitz   Ramon Ziai   Kordula De Kuthy   Detmar Meurers
Seminar für Sprachwissenschaft, SFB 833, LEAD
Universität Tübingen
{brzdwtz,rziai,kdk,dm}@sfs.uni-tuebingen.de

Abstract

We discuss the development of FeedBook, an intelligent electronic workbook supporting the teaching of English as Foreign Language in German secondary school. The overarching goal is to address real-life formal education needs using current Natural Language Processing technology.

Our interactive, web-based workbook is based on the print workbook of a schoolbook officially approved for 7th grade English classes in secondary schools in Baden-Württemberg, Germany. The workbook offers a range of activities for students that typically are assigned by instructors as homework to accompany the regular English classes. In our web-based version, students can complete activities online, submit them to their teacher, and view teacher feedback. Teachers are supported in providing both formative and summative feedback to individual students by an auto-correct and feedback memory system, and they can view aggregates of student performance.

This article describes the development of the web-based workbook and its use from a technical and pedagogical perspective. We are currently working on adding automatic immediate feedback to learners that is designed to incrementally support individual learners in successfully completing a given task.

1   Introduction

Research in Second Language Acquisition (SLA) and Foreign Language Teaching (FLT) has stressed the importance of individualized, immediate feedback on learner production for learner proficiency development (e.g., Mackey, 2006). In the classroom, the teacher is generally the only source of reliable, accurate feedback available to students, which poses a well-known practical problem: in a class of 30 students, despite individual differences warranting individual feedback to students, it is highly challenging for a teacher to provide it in class or, in a timely fashion, on homework.

One of the means to address this problem are Intelligent Tutoring Systems (ITS), which have been advocated since the 90's. Such systems are successfully used in domains such as mathematics (Sabo et al., 2013), where the system input can be sufficiently constrained to support automatic evaluation. In the language domain, ITS are much less common, although there has been extensive related research (cf., Heift and Schulze, 2007).

In order to address the gap between research on intelligent language tutors, foreign language teaching insights, and real-life classroom usage, we are developing FeedBook, a web-based English workbook we are creating in collaboration with Diesterweg of the Westermann Gruppe, a major German schoolbook publisher.[1] The ultimate goal of the system is to provide individualized and immediate scaffolding feedback to learners in order to guide them towards solutions for a number of different activities. In the current stage, the system provides a web-based implementation of the traditional print workbook which enables students to complete activities and teachers to give formative and summative feedback on the language produced by the student. The teacher is assisted through several automatic mechanisms, ranging from the system remembering previously given feedback to annotation suggestions based on Natural Language Processing (NLP) technology.

---

[1] https://verlage.westermanngruppe.de

Björn Rudzewitz, Ramon Ziai, Kordula De Kuthy and Detmar Meurers 2017. Developing a web-based workbook for English supporting the interaction of students and teachers. *Proceedings of the Joint 6th Workshop on NLP for Computer Assisted Language Learning and 2nd Workshop on NLP for Research on Language Acquisition at NoDaLiDa 2017.* Linköping Electronic Conference Proceedings 134: 36–46.

The paper is organized as follows: Section 2 briefly discusses some existing language tutoring approaches. In section 3, we discuss the challenges involved in creating a web-based workbook based on a traditional print workbook. Section 4 then discusses FeedBook and its different components in detail, before section 5 concludes the paper with an outlook on next steps of the project.

2 Related Work

Intelligent Language Tutoring Systems (ILTS) proposed in the literature range from highly ambitious conversation machines (e.g., DeSmedt, 1995) to more modest workbook-like approaches (e.g., Heift and Nicholson, 2001; Nagata, 2002). However, as discussed by Heift and Schulze (2007), most of the systems are research prototypes that have never seen real-life testing or use. Following Amaral and Meurers (2011), we describe three notable exceptions below.

Robo-Sensei (Nagata, 2009) is a system for Japanese which presents a series of exercises for each of its 24 lessons. The activities are contextualized, including visual aids and picture material on Japan. The system was created by Noriko Nagata, who also designed the Japanese teaching curriculum. The effectiveness of the system has been investigated explicitly (Nagata, 1993; 1996; 1997), confirming that *Robo-Sensei* supports the acquisition of grammar and vocabulary. *Robo-Sensei* generally constrains the language that the learner enters into the system by providing English cues, thus essentially presenting contextualized translation exercises.

The *E-Tutor* (Heift, 2003) is an ILTS for German developed by Trude Heift and integrated into the German curriculum of her department at Simon Fraser University. German students in the program complete *E-Tutor* exercises as regular class requirement, which has enabled Trude Heift to research the system's effectiveness and further its development (Heift, 2001; 2004; 2005). The system contains four types of exercises with NLP support: *i)* provide the missing word, *ii)* build sentences with the words given, *iii)* translate a phrase, and *iv)* write down the sentence read by the system. The exercise types explicitly constrain the learner productions through the words and phrases given in the prompt.

TAGARELA (Amaral and Meurers, 2011) is a tutor system for Portuguese. It is a web-based workbook featuring six activity types: listening comprehension, reading comprehension, rephrasing, description, fill-in-the-blanks and vocabulary practice. The system was integrated into the Portuguese program at The Ohio State University and the University of Massachusetts Amherst, where Luiz Amaral integrated it into individualized instruction, regular courses, and distance learning courses. Some of the activity types explicitly constrain the learner productions, whereas the comprehension tasks attempt to do so implicitly through the contents. To make the system more flexible in terms of activity types and user demands, a modular architecture based on UIMA (Ferrucci and Lally, 2004) was developed (Amaral et al., 2011), including a complete rewrite of the NLP components.

Overall, there have been only few attempts to connect state-of-the-art NLP and insights from SLA with actual widespread classroom usage, and the developers of the tutoring system were also involved in the actual teaching.

3 Adapting a Print Workbook for the Web

In contrast to the related work just discussed, the system introduced here takes as starting point an existing workbook that already is integrated into the real-life formal education context. To accomplish the goal of improving the learning experience for the students and support the teachers with minimal overhead, a crucial requirement for our development was to make the digital version as similar as possible to the look and feel to the print version. Users familiar with the print workbook thus can directly benefit from the added value of the web-based version without first requiring training.[2]

The web-based workbook is based on the print version of the schoolbook *Camden Town Gymnasium 3*, approved for 7th grade English classes in German secondary schools. As a first step moving from a print workbook to a web-based version, it is necessary to decide which activities to include and what a general data model representing them should look like. We therefore analyzed and categorized all activities in the print schoolbook in order to group similar exercises together and form a category system that generalizes over all group

---

[2]To be able to address any issues arising in real-life use, the system also includes the functionality to contact the developers with bugs or feature requests.

Proceedings of the Joint 6th Workshop on NLP for Computer Assisted Language Learning and 2nd Workshop on NLP for Research on Language Acquisition at NoDaLiDa 2017

instances. To this end, we analyzed all activities of the print workbook in terms of:

(i) activity type, e.g., reading comprehension, fill-in-the-blank

(ii) expected well- or ill-formed language variation: How is the space of possible learner productions restricted by the instruction and material (cf. Quixal and Meurers, 2016; Meurers and Dickinson, 2017)

(iii) expected type of system input, e.g., check marks, single characters, words, a sentence, short texts

(iv) form or meaning-orientation

(v) language forms targeted explicitly or implicitly, e.g., simple past vs. past perfect.

Given our overall goal of linking real-life needs to NLP-based solutions, our primary focus is on activities for which the learners produce language (as opposed to, e.g., check marks), but where the language produced is constrained enough to determine potential reference answers (which rules out, e.g., activities asking about the students' background). We also aimed to cover both meaning- and form-oriented tasks, as both aspects are essential in FLT and contained in current workbooks.

Development first concentrated on two activity types: short answers (requiring one or more free-text sentences, usually in a meaning-oriented activity), and fill-in-the-blanks (a text with gaps, usually lexical content or form-oriented). Since some of the activities we chose also contain preparatory sub-tasks involving mapping (text or images that need to be matched) or variants of multiple-choice, we also included those task types to be able to offer the same activity sequences as in the print workbook. We currently cover 55 of the 177 workbook activities (some containing preparatory sub-tasks). To support a systematic use of the web-based workbook as a straightforward replacement of the print version in real-life teaching, we are currently adding further activity types. As also argued in Amaral and Meurers (2011), satisfying real-life education needs using an ILTS is as dependent on the user interface, web-programming, and related visual and task design issues as it is on the NLP analysis.

Figure 1 provides an example task from the *Camden Town 3* print workbook, where students are asked to watch a video clip provided on a DVD and answer questions.[3] In Figure 4, we will later see the web-based adaptation of the same task.

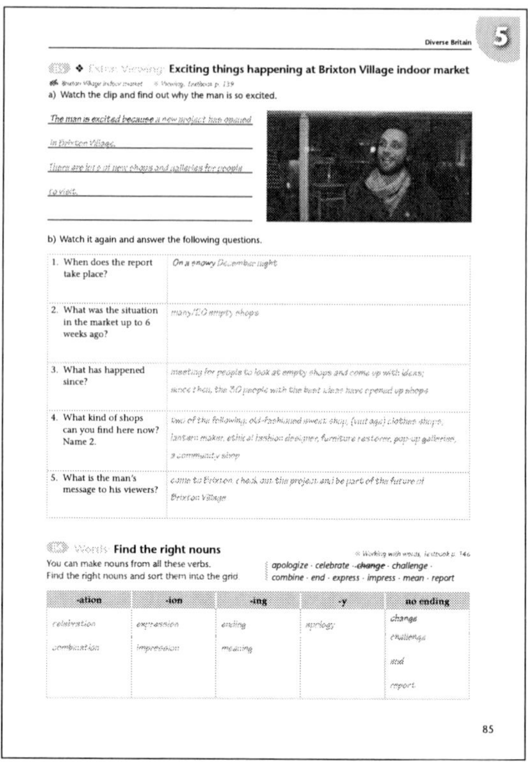

Figure 1: Example task from the print workbook © *Westermann Gruppe*

Following common software engineering practice, in FeedBook we separate display from function and content. The display of an activity is determined by its activity type rather than being hard-coded for individual activities. This readily supports adding activities of the established types at a later point by providing only the new content. This implies that the data model for activities contains both textual content as well as links to context media such as graphics or audio. The activity data model also integrates all components required for the NLP analysis to provide feedback. For example, for processing short answers in terms of the semantic appropriateness, the feedback system needs direct access to the prompt text (reading question), the target answer, and the student answer (cf., e.g., Meurers et al., 2011b).

In the next section, we present the FeedBook functionality and how it integrates the activities and challenges characterized in this section.

---

[3]In this teacher version of the workbook, target answers are shown in green.

4   The FeedBook System

The FeedBook is designed as a multi-layer web application. The system is platform-independent, only requiring a computer, tablet, or smartphone with a web browser and internet access. The current version of the system supports a common workflow in German secondary schools: Students work on exercises, typically after being assigned those exercises as homework by the teacher, and submit their results to the teacher. The teacher corrects the submission and sends it back to the student with the feedback. The system provides automatic error annotation assistance and a feedback memory to facilitate the work of the teacher. The student can inspect the teacher feedback, and a diagnostics interface allows the teacher to identify general problems. Since the system is currently used by German students at a lower to intermediate level of English proficiency, German is used as interface and meta language, though this can be configured differently.

The purpose of the FeedBook is *not* to replace the class or the teachers, but to provide an opportunity for students to individually practice using online exercises at any time. It also relieves teachers from the repetitive work of providing feedback on the same issues over and over again, while at the same time allowing them to view aggregates of student performance so that they can use the class time efficiently to target common issues or misconceptions.

In the following, the system as developed in the first phase of the project is described in more detail, following the workflow just outlined. While for the second phase of the project, we are working on system components that provide immediate individual scaffolding feedback to students while they work on the activities, the teacher feedback data currently being collected is already used to reduce the work load of the teacher through components included in the discussion below.

4.1   The Lobby

The lobby is the central starting point loaded after a standard authentication process requiring a user name and password. The structure and functionality of the lobby differs by the role of the user (teacher, student, administrator) who logged in to accommodate their different needs.

Student Lobby   For students, the lobby presents a table of contents hosting all exercises as tiles in a mosaic design grouped by the book themes. Figure 2 shows the lobby after selection of Theme 5 "Diverse Britain".

After a student worked on an exercise, the exercise tile with the exercise title and page number[4] also indicates whether an exercise has been saved by the student, submitted to the teacher, or corrected by the teacher. In the latter case, a check mark using a traffic light color scheme indicates the overall teacher rating, and an information symbol indicates that the teacher provided annotations of errors or other comments.

When clicking on or touching an exercise tile, FeedBook forwards the student to the Practice Interface (section 4.2) or to the Result Interface showing feedback (section 4.4), depending on the state of the exercise.

Teacher Lobby   Teachers have a choice between two conceptually and functionally distinct variants of the lobby: (a) tree view, (b) submission table.

In variant (a), the teacher is shown the two column layout illustrated in Figure 3). In the left column, a table of contents of the workbook is shown, including only activities to which submissions of the teacher's students exist. On selection of an activity, a submission table is shown in the right column listing all associated students (the class), the time they submitted the activity, their detailed submission status (correction pending, partially corrected, correction complete), the number of error annotations added to this submission, and the overall rating. Selecting a submission via click or touch forwards the teacher to the correction view (section 4.4).[5]

In variant (b), the teacher sees a list widget with all submissions. This includes all of the information mentioned above, but for all submitted exercises. The list can be filtered to only show submission that still require teacher interaction so that this view can serve as a To-Do list for teachers. This view also permits direct selection of submissions by click or touch.

Two buttons are shown at the table bottom. The first serves to automatically mark all submissions that are identical to the target answers provided by the teacher workbook as correct. The second button sends a reminder to all student who have not yet submitted the exercise.

---

[4]The page number is included for ease of cross-reference with the print workbook.

[5]Teachers can revisit and revise corrections incrementally.

Proceedings of the Joint 6th Workshop on NLP for Computer Assisted Language Learning and 2nd Workshop on NLP for Research on Language Acquisition at NoDaLiDa 2017

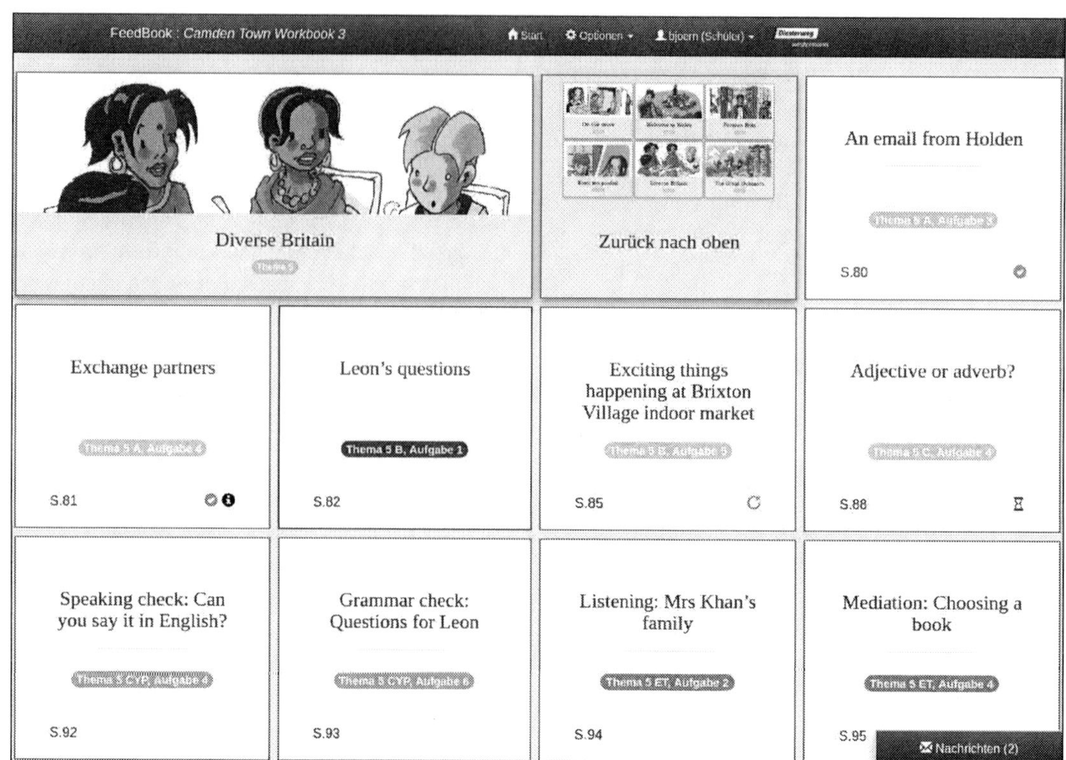

Figure 2: Student Lobby

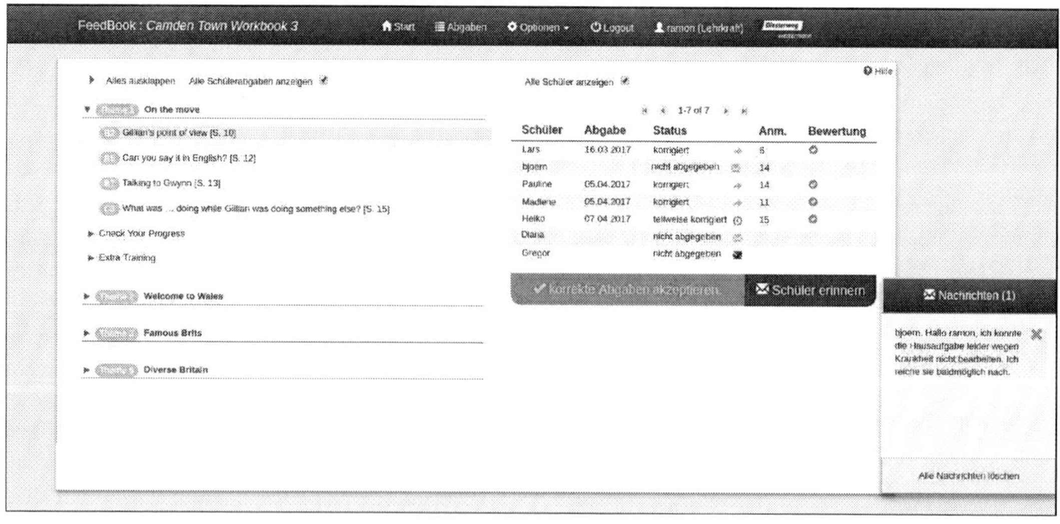

Figure 3: Teacher Lobby

4.2 The Practice Interface for Students

The Practice Interface offers a fully functional web-based version of an exercise to students. For the print workbook exercise we saw in Figure 1, the web-based version is shown in Figure 4.

Figure 4: Student Practice Interface

The type of interactive input elements shown depends on the exercise type. If the workbook provides example answers, as often is the case for the first input field, these are visualized differently (unless the student changes them). If an exercise consists of multiple sub-tasks, the student can navigate freely between them. For all exercise types, the student has the functionality to save intermediate results and resume the exercise and all sub-tasks with any system input the student has provided for any number of trials. Once a student submits an exercise, the student is redirected to the lobby and the exercise is locked until the teacher has corrected it in the feedback interface.

4.3 The Feedback Interface for Teachers

The Feedback Interface is where the teacher has the opportunity to give feedback to student input on workbook activities. Starting out from the teacher lobby discussed in section 4.1, the teacher can view and select student submissions to particular activities. Once a student submission has been selected, the Feedback interface loads, rendering the student input in the context of the respective activity, in a view similar to the Practice Interface shown in Figure 4.

The teacher can then give both formative and summative feedback. The latter is given for the whole activity in the form of a star rating (1–5) and an optional global comment. Formative feedback can consist of specific annotations of the learner submission. Given its relevance to the overall goal of the FeedBook, we here describe it in more detail. In order to add an annotation, the teacher can select any sub-span of the student production, which opens the error annotation dialog shown in Figure 5.

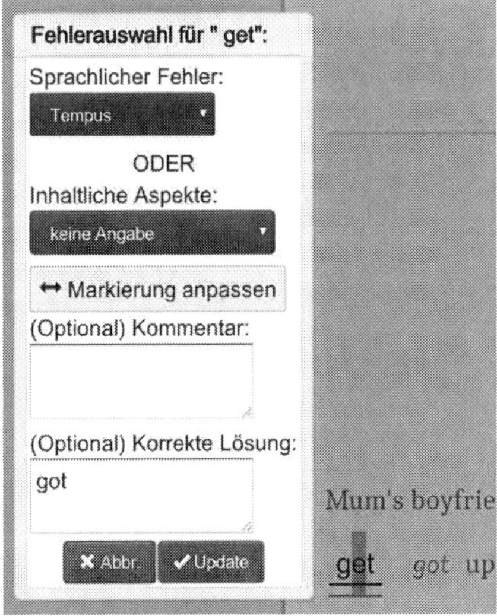

Figure 5: The error annotation dialog

In this dialog, the teacher can specify four different characteristics: (i) the extent (span) of the error, (ii) the error type describing the nature of divergence from the norm, (iii) an example of a correct solution, and (iv) a free-text comment on this annotation. The error types we use are based on the categories provided by teachers in a pilot study. We grouped them into language form and content errors, as spelled out in Table 1.

Language form errors	Content errors
phrasing, agreement,	problematic understanding,
determiner, preposition,	missing information,
grammar, spelling,	wrong information,
pronoun, tense,	lack of understanding,
clause structure,	extra information,
word choice, missing word,	alternate answer
word order, punctuation	

Table 1: Error types in FeedBook

The annotations are saved in the database along with the student productions. They can be retrieved by several system components, in particular the Result Interface for students discussed in section 4.4.

4.3.1 Automatic Error Annotation Assistance

To assist teachers in providing feedback and reduce their workload, the FeedBook provides three distinct mechanisms: (i) a visual comparison with a pre-stored target response, (ii) a feedback memory storing the history of previously given feedback, and (iii) an automatic error annotation approach for some of the errors in the system. We discuss each of these features below.

Visual Highlighting of Answer Divergence In the current version of the system, each student answer is first string-matched against the pre-stored target answer; more complex matching approaches building on the research strands we compare in Ott et al. (2013) will be explored later in the project. If the match is positive, the student answer is assumed to be correct and no further processing needs to take place. This outcome is visualized to the teacher in the form of a green check mark next to the student answer.

If the answers differ from each other, a diff-like algorithm exemplified in Figure 6 is employed to find and highlight the parts of the student answer that differ from the target answer. This is done on two levels: First, for each target answer token, the nearest student answer token is identified via edit distance (Damerau, 1964). After this alignment step, the words thus matched are compared on a character level, and the differences in the student answer are highlighted. In order to avoid visualizing random meaningless similarities, highlighting is only performed if half the target answer material was identified in the student answer.

Mum's boyfriend was coming to meet me so of course I

get   *got* up in a bad mood. But Mum giving

gave me a great big smile. She made ✓ me my

favourite pancakes with maple syrup for breakfast but I

wasn't ✓ hungry. She tries *tried* to cheer me up

and say *suggested* that we go shopping. That usually

Figure 6: Difference highlighting example

Feedback Memory Depending on the activity type, many students will provide the same or very similar solutions to a given prompt. This is especially the case for more constrained types of activities. Ideally, the teacher should only have to provide feedback to such student answers once, and the system should remember previously given feedback to a given prompt and present it to the teacher at correction time. FeedBook achieves this by querying its database for feedback to the same prompts when the Feedback Interface is loaded, filling in any error annotations found for learner answers that were already annotated. This achieves both a reduction of the teacher's workload and a higher consistency in the teacher's error annotation.

Auto-correction In case there is no previous feedback from teachers, FeedBook provides automatic suggestions to the teacher based on NLP techniques. Eventually, this functionality will cover all activity and error types in the system, paving the way towards providing immediate feedback directly to the learner while they work on the exercise.

As a first step, we have implemented fine-grained feedback on the word level for grammatical errors in fill-in-the-blank activities. In order to perform error analysis reliably, the target answers are processed ahead of time in an NLP pipeline consisting of tokenization, sentence detection, POS tagging, lemmatization, morphological analysis, and dependency parsing. We use the Unstructured Information Management Architecture (UIMA, Ferrucci and Lally, 2004) along with the DKPro component repository (de Castilho and Gurevych, 2014), which provides access to many state-of-the-art NLP tools within an industry-strength processing framework supporting multiple layers of annotation. Table 2 lists the NLP components we use.

NLP task	Component Used
Tokenization, Sentence Detection, POS tagging	NLP Toolkit for JVM Languages (NLP4J[6])
Lemmatization	Morpha (Minnen et al., 2001)
Morphology	SFST with EMOR model (Schmid, 2005; Karp et al., 1992)
Dependency Parsing	MaltParser (Nivre et al., 2007)

Table 2: NLP components used in auto-correction

The automatically annotated linguistic information in the target answers is then manually post-corrected in order to provide a solid basis of reliable linguistic information for error diagnosis. We use WebAnno (Eckart de Castilho et al., 2016) for this purpose, which readily supports inspection and annotation of linguistic information produced by DKPro components.

When the teacher selects the Feedback Interface, the student answers are processed analogously to the target answers. On the basis of the annotated target answers, a sequence of rules compares student and target answer on different linguistic levels to determine the nature of the divergence to identify a non-word, a different POS, or a different inflection. This information on the divergence is then used as evidence for specific error annotations, such as *spelling*, *wrong word* or *tense* error. The first rule that applies stops the process, so once an error type has been identified, no more sophisticated comparisons are attempted.

In case we cannot diagnose the nature of the error, a default error category is annotated, which is visually distinguished in the Feedback interface. The teacher can post-edit any automatically generated error annotations and change or remove them. In such cases of manual intervention, the system stores the now manually corrected annotations as instances for the Feedback Memory mechanism.

4.4 The Result Interface for Students

In the Result Interface, students see the selected activity with their submitted answers. Next to each student answer, the teacher's annotations are displayed if present. At the bottom, the system shows the global rating and comments by the teacher. In this interface, the student sees almost the same as the teacher in the Feedback Interface, the difference being that annotations are not editable and target answers are not shown (unless they were included by the teacher in the feedback).

4.5 The Diagnostics Interface

Teachers have access to a Diagnostics Interface, illustrated in Figure 7. After selecting a specific activity or an activity type, FeedBook offers three visualizations: A bar chart shows the quantitative distribution of annotations (errors) over the error categories introduced in section 4.3. This makes it possible to identify frequent problems

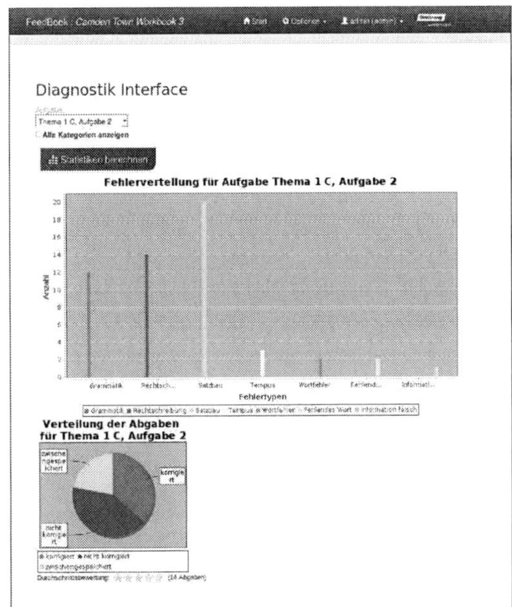

Figure 7: Diagnostics Interface

in an exercise at one glance. Teachers can then use their class time more effectively to target these problems. For publishers this type of information would also be valuable for determining whether the errors made by students correlate with the pedagogical goal of the given activity or whether there are problems in the design of the exercise leading to unintended errors.

The interface also contains a pie chart showing the distribution of the submission status for an exercise, i.e., what percentage of students worked on the exercise so far, how many exercises were submitted and await being corrected, and how many were already corrected. This chart thus serves as a progress indicator for a given exercise.

Finally, the Diagnostics Interface provides a visualization of the average global rating that the teacher gave to the submissions to a given exercise and the number of instances this is based on. The cases where students perform extremely low or high are especially interesting because they indicate a mismatch between the students' abilities and the activity demands.

4.6 Communication and Administration

For a web-based workbook, some communication and administration functionality is needed.

News System The FeedBook comes with a messaging service. For each activity submitted to a

---

[6]https://emorynlp.github.io/nlp4j

Proceedings of the Joint 6th Workshop on NLP for Computer Assisted Language Learning and 2nd Workshop on NLP for Research on Language Acquisition at NoDaLiDa 2017

teacher, the student is shown a confirmation message in the news feed. When a teacher has corrected an activity, the student receives a clickable message, which will forward the student to the Result Interface for this exercise. Furthermore, teachers can write messages to each of their students, students can write to their teacher, and administrators can send messages to everyone. In the message, the name of the sender is shown.

The news feed widget always pops up in the lobby in case new (unread) messages exist, and the messages can be deleted by the recipient with a click on a cross displayed next to the text.

Account Management As the very first step in working with the FeedBook, teachers need to create accounts for their students. Student accounts can be created in a batch with the option to auto-generate passwords and to print the individual account information for distribution to the students in class. Once accounts exist, teachers have the possibility to reset their students' passwords in the account management interface in case a student forgets the credentials. Users can also change their own password. Teacher accounts are created by an admin user.

4.7 Meeting the Requirements of a Modern Web Application

Cross-Device Optimization To provide a convenient and motivating user experience encouraging users to interact with FeedBook, the system uses state-of-the-art web technology. A web application needs to provide an optimized display for all devices and platforms ranging from small mobile phones to wide monitors. For this, not only the size but also the positioning of elements needs to be adjusted. To build a fully scalable application, we use the Bootstrap[7] framework and its grid system for the display layer. We imitate a paper sheet via a stylized virtual paper as background that scales to all devices, in contrast to, for example, a PDF with a static width. Another challenge is to make the system work with mouse and keyboard input as well as with touch screens. For instance, in the Feedback Interface, where the teachers needs to select spans of the student answer, an additional selection slider menu is shown for touch events to support the same functionality available using a mouse.

Navigation The FeedBook features a permanently accessible navigation bar attached to the screen top. Among the functionality universal to all user groups it supports redirection to the lobby ("Start"), access to account management, and further options for some user groups. Teachers can navigate to the alternative lobby view ("Abgaben") discussed in section 4.1, and the options menu sports different drop-down menu items depending on the user group needs. The amount of information and the verbosity changes depending on the screen size, from a fully textual to an iconified mobile-friendly version for smaller devices.

5 Summary and Outlook

We presented the FeedBook, a web-based adaptation of a print workbook for English in 7th grade that aims at individually supporting students in completing both meaning- and form-based exercises. In the current stage, the system relies on the teacher to provide the feedback, but already considerably reduces the teacher workload through automatic visual highlighting, a feedback memory, and NLP-supported automatic error annotation suggestions. Moreover, the design of Feed-Book as an online platform where students and teachers directly interact outside of the classroom enables teachers to flexibly assign activities and provide feedback.

The first version of FeedBook has been in use in pilot classrooms since October 2016 and feedback from teachers and students has been very supportive. We have put a premium on integrating feedback for new features and bug fixes in a timely fashion to ensure that the system continuously meets the demands of real-life classroom usage. For demonstration purposes, a separate instance of the system is available on the project website[8].

We are currently working on automating feedback for more types of student input as suggestions for the teachers. This will involve more complex NLP, especially for short answer tasks and content errors. In this context, we are exploring integration of a state-of-the-art short answer assessment system such as CoMiC (Meurers et al., 2011a) into the FeedBook.

In the next phase of the project, we will move the burden of giving feedback from the teacher to the system and redesign the FeedBook to provide

---

[7]http://getbootstrap.com

[8]http://feedback.website

Proceedings of the Joint 6th Workshop on NLP for Computer Assisted Language Learning and 2nd Workshop on NLP for Research on Language Acquisition at NoDaLiDa 2017

immediate, scaffolding feedback while the learner is completing the activity. The feedback data gathered from teachers up to this point will clearly be important for this development, and we will continue to give teachers the possibility to revise automatic feedback and provide manual feedback. In the third year of the project, we plan to conduct a randomized controlled field study integrating measures of the process and product of learning. We plan to compare the web-based workbook providing automated feedback with a web-based workbook transmitting only the teacher-provided feedback in order to evaluate the impact of immediate, scaffolding feedback on learning outcomes and motivation.

Acknowledgments

We gratefully acknowledge the support of this knowledge transfer project SFB833/T1 through the DFG. We would like to thank Christoph Golla and Laura Lanik, our project partners at the Westermann Gruppe, for the good cooperation. The project would also not be possible without the substantial contribution of the student research assistants: Verena Blaschke, Jekaterina Kaparina, Madeesh Kannan, Maxim Korniyenko, Johannes Krämer, Mai Mayeg, Samantha Tureski, Tobias Pütz, and Kuan Yu.

References

Luiz Amaral and Detmar Meurers. 2011. On using intelligent computer-assisted language learning in real-life foreign language teaching and learning. *ReCALL*, 23(1):4–24.

Luiz Amaral, Detmar Meurers, and Ramon Ziai. 2011. Analyzing learner language: Towards a flexible NLP architecture for intelligent language tutors. *Computer-Assisted Language Learning*, 24(1):1–16.

Fred J. Damerau. 1964. A technique for computer detection and correction of errors. *Communications of the ACM*, 7:171–176.

Richard Eckart de Castilho and Iryna Gurevych. 2014. A broad-coverage collection of portable NLP components for building shareable analysis pipelines. In *Proceedings of the Workshop on Open Infrastructures and Analysis Frameworks for HLT (OIAF4HLT) at COLING 2014*, pages 1–11, Dublin, Ireland. ACL and Dublin City University.

William DeSmedt. 1995. Herr Kommissar: An ICALL conversation simulator for intermediate German. In V. Melissa Holland, Jonathan Kaplan, and Michelle Sams, editors, *Intelligent Language Tutors: Theory Shaping Technology*, pages 153–174. Lawrence Erlbaum Associates Inc., New Jersey.

Richard Eckart de Castilho, Éva Mújdricza-Maydt, Muhie Seid Yimam, Silvana Hartmann, Iryna Gurevych, Anette Frank, and Chris Biemann. 2016. A web-based tool for the integrated annotation of semantic and syntactic structures. In *Proceedings of the Workshop on Language Technology Resources and Tools for Digital Humanities (LT4DH)*, pages 76–84.

David Ferrucci and Adam Lally. 2004. UIMA: An architectural approach to unstructured information processing in the corporate research environment. *Natural Language Engineering*, 10(3–4):327–348.

Trude Heift and Devlan Nicholson. 2001. Web delivery of adaptive and interactive language tutoring. *International Journal of Artificial Intelligence in Education*, 12(4):310–325.

Trude Heift and Mathias Schulze. 2007. *Errors and Intelligence in Computer-Assisted Language Learning: Parsers and Pedagogues*. Routledge.

Trude Heift. 2001. Error-specific and individualized feedback in a web-based language tutoring system: Do they read it? *ReCALL*, 13(2):129–142.

Trude Heift. 2003. Multiple learner errors and meaningful feedback: A challenge for ICALL systems. *CALICO Journal*, 20(3):533–548.

Trude Heift. 2004. Corrective feedback and learner uptake in call. *ReCALL*, 16(2):416–431.

Trude Heift. 2005. Inspectable learner reports for web-based language learning. *ReCALL*, 17(1):32–46.

Daniel Karp, Yves Schabes, Martin Zaidel, and Dania Egedi. 1992. A freely available wide coverage morphological analyzer for English. In *Proceedings of the 14th Conference on Computational Linguistics*, COLING '92, pages 950–955, Stroudsburg, PA.

Alison Mackey. 2006. Feedback, noticing and instructed second language learning. *Applied Linguistics*, 27(3):405–430.

Detmar Meurers and Markus Dickinson. 2017. Evidence and interpretation in language learning research: Opportunities for collaboration with computational linguistics. *Language Learning*, 67(2). http://dx.doi.org/10.1111/lang.12233.

Detmar Meurers, Ramon Ziai, Niels Ott, and Stacey Bailey. 2011a. Integrating parallel analysis modules to evaluate the meaning of answers to reading comprehension questions. *IJCEELL. Special Issue on Automatic Free-text Evaluation*, 21(4):355–369.

Detmar Meurers, Ramon Ziai, Niels Ott, and Janina Kopp. 2011b. Evaluating answers to reading comprehension questions in context: Results for German and the role of information structure. In *Proceedings of the TextInfer 2011 Workshop on Textual Entailment*, pages 1–9, Edinburgh.

Guido Minnen, John Carroll, and Darren Pearce. 2001. Applied morphological processing of English. *Natural Language Engineering*, 7(3):207–233.

Noriko Nagata. 1993. Intelligent computer feedback for second language instruction. *The Modern Language Journal*, 77(3):330–339.

Noriko Nagata. 1996. Computer vs. workbook instruction in second language acquistion. *CALICO Journal*, 14(1):53–75.

Noriko Nagata. 1997. The effectiveness of computer-assisted metalinguistic instruction: A case study in Japanese. *Foreign Language Annals*, 30(2):187–200.

Noriko Nagata. 2002. BANZAI: An application of natural language processing to web-based language learning. *CALICO Journal*, 19(3):583–599.

Noriko Nagata. 2009. Robo-Sensei's NLP-based error detection and feedback generation. *CALICO Journal*, 26(3):562–579.

Joakim Nivre, Jens Nilsson, Johan Hall, Atanas Chanev, Gülsen Eryigit, Sandra Kübler, Svetoslav Marinov, and Erwin Marsi. 2007. MaltParser: A language-independent system for data-driven dependency parsing. *Natural Language Engineering*, 13(1):1–41.

Niels Ott, Ramon Ziai, Michael Hahn, and Detmar Meurers. 2013. CoMeT: Integrating different levels of linguistic modeling for meaning assessment. In *Proceedings of the 7th International Workshop on Semantic Evaluation (SemEval)*, pages 608–616, Atlanta, GA. ACL.

Martí Quixal and Detmar Meurers. 2016. How can writing tasks be characterized in a way serving pedagogical goals and automatic analysis needs? *CALICO Journal*, 33:19–48.

Kent E. Sabo, Robert K. Atkinson, Angela L. Barrus, Stacey S. Joseph, and Ray S. Perez. 2013. Searching for the two sigma advantage: Evaluating algebra intelligent tutors. *Computers in Human Behavior*, 29(4):1833–1840.

Helmut Schmid. 2005. A programming language for finite state transducers. In *Proceedings of the 5th International Workshop on Finite State Methods in Natural Language Processing (FSMNLP)*, pages 308–309.

Annotating Errors in Student Texts: First Experiences and Experiments

Sara Stymne, Eva Pettersson, Beáta Megyesi
Linguistics and Philology
Uppsala University
`first_name.last_name@lingfil.uu.se`

Anne Palmér
Scandinavian Languages
Uppsala University
`anne.palmer@nordiska.uu.se`

Abstract

We describe the creation of an annotation layer for word-based writing errors for a corpus of student writings. The texts are written in Swedish by students between 9 and 19 years old. Our main purpose is to identify errors regarding spelling, split compounds and merged words. In addition, we also identify simple word-based grammatical errors, including morphological errors and extra words. In this paper we describe the corpus and the annotation process, including detailed descriptions of the error types and guidelines. We find that we can perform this annotation with a substantial inter-annotator agreement, but that there are still some remaining issues with the annotation. We also report results on two pilot experiments regarding spelling correction and the consistency of downstream NLP tools, to exemplify the usefulness of the annotated corpus.

1 Introduction

The use of automatic tools for the detection and correction of writing errors is not new, and there are many tools that can accurately correct errors in standard texts in many languages, including Swedish. However, most of the existing tools are not freely available and usually do not provide any information on the error type. Automatic grammatical correction of texts written by language learners, especially second language learners is even more problematic with various types of errors.

In order to investigate language learning processes, to give students feedback, and to develop computer-assisted language learning and teaching applications (ICALL) by using NLP tools like taggers and parsers for automatic analysis of non-standard texts, it is important to be able to identify and classify various types of grammatical errors. Data collection and analysis by creating a corpus on learner language with annotation on various linguistic layers from part-of-speech (POS) to syntactic analysis is a first step. In parallel to corpus creation, tools can be developed for the automatic processing of learner data which can be used for analysis of new texts.

In this paper we present the development of a corpus on learner language of Swedish, the Uppsala Corpus of Student Writings (Megyesi et al., 2016) by creating a normalization layer identifying erroneous constructions on top of an already existing automatic linguistic annotation. In this work humans annotate word-based errors focusing on spelling, split compounds, merged words, and simple grammatical errors. The original corpus includes 2,500 student writings from different age groups and grades, written by students who study Swedish (L1) or Swedish as a second language (L2). The group of students who study Swedish as a school language consists both of native Swedish speakers, and non-native speakers who have a good command of Swedish, and those essays thus contain texts written both by L1 and L2 speakers. We describe the creation of the annotation layer for normalization for a subset of this corpus and perform two initial experiments, exemplifying how this corpus can be used.

The corpus presented is intended to be useful for researchers in computational linguistics as well as for scholars interested in student writings and assessment of Swedish as L1 and/or L2. From a computational linguistics perspective, the data will allow us to develop, train, and evaluate models for error identification and correction that are particularly geared towards student writings in Swedish,

Sara Stymne, Eva Pettersson, Beáta Megyesi and Anne Palmér 2017. Annotating errors in student texts: First experiences and experiments. *Proceedings of the Joint 6th Workshop on NLP for Computer Assisted Language Learning and 2nd Workshop on NLP for Research on Language Acquisition at NoDaLiDa 2017.* Linköping Electronic Conference Proceedings 134: 47–60.

possibly also adapting the models to different age groups, levels, and for students of Swedish as L1 or L2. Being able to correct errors is also important in order to achieve good performance on downstream tasks like tagging and parsing. From a writing development perspective, the normalized corpus can allow analysis of writing skills development during school years in Swedish as L1 or L2. The error identification accomplished in this corpus is also interesting from an assessment and grading perspective, and can contribute to the development of advanced computer-assisted language learning and teaching applications.

2 Related Work

In research on student writing, correctness of the text is considered as one of several aspects measuring writing development and text quality. However, there is not a simple relationship between correctness and writing development. In second language writing, for example, it is well known that correctness and complexity of language are balancing factors. When focusing on correctness the student may write a less complex text, and a text with a more complex language — showing a higher level of linguistic development — may contain more errors, see e.g. Axelsson and Magnusson (2012) or Abrahamsson and Bergman (2014)).

Learner corpora allowing research studies on language learning have been available for several languages, e.g for English (Hawkins and Buttery, 2010), Norwegian (Tenfjord et al., 2004), Italian, German and Czech (Hana et al., 2004) and (Abel et al., 2014), as well as for Swedish, such as ASU (Hammarberg, 2005), CrossCheck (Lindberg and Eriksson, 2004), Swedish EALA (Saxena and Borin, 2002), and SweLL (Volodina et al., 2016). While there are hundreds of learner corpora today for various languages, only a few of them are annotated with error types along with linguistic analysis. ASK – the Norwegian Second Language Corpus (Tenfjord et al., 2004) is one important Scandinavian source including 10 different native languages, annotated for errors and partly parsed. Nicholls (2003) describes the error coding and performs an analysis of the annotation of the Cambridge Learner Corpus, consisting of texts written in English by learners. She describes a scheme for inline annotations of a comprehensive set of errors. Like us, they aim to preserve both the original text and to have a corrected ver-

sion. A part of this corpus has been manually annotated with POS-tags and dependency structures, and was recently released as the Treebank of Learner English (Berzak et al., 2016).

In the spell checking and grammar checking literature, e.g. Brill and Moore (2000) or Carlberger et al. (2005), corpora with annotated errors are often used for evaluation. However, little is usually written about these annotations.

3 Corpus Data

3.1 The Uppsala Corpus of Student Writings

Megyesi et al. (2016) presented the Uppsala Corpus of Student Writings (UCSW), which consists of essays written as part of Swedish national tests for schools in the subjects Swedish and Swedish as a second language. The corpus contains essays written by students in different grades, ranging from year three in primary school (at age nine) to year three in upper secondary school (at age nineteen). The tests have been collected since 1996. The texts arc digitized versions either of handwritten essays, or of printed essays that have been scanned. The full corpus consists of 2,500 essays containing more than 1.5 million tokens today but the corpus is intended to be a monitor corpus, extended with new, analyzed tests.

The texts in UCSW are annotated automatically in a pipeline using SweGram (Näsman et al., 2017), an online tool for automatic analysis of Swedish texts. The tool includes tokenization, normalization to correct spelling errors and split compounds, part-of-speech tagging, and dependency parsing. First tokenization is performed to separate sentences and tokens, using the Svannotate tool (Nivre et al., 2008). Then spelling errors are corrected by using a simple unweighted Levenshtein distance, with threshold 1 on all unknown words (Pettersson et al., 2013). Split compounds are addressed by using a set of a few rules (Öhrman, 1998). Part-of-speech tagging and morphological analysis are carried out using efselab (Östling, 2016) and dependency parsing is performed using MaltParser (Nivre et al., 2006). The analysis tools achieve state-of-the-art accuracy on standard texts with the exception of the normalizer. The corrections of spelling errors and split compounds are very noisy and far from human quality, thus necessitating work on these issues.

USCW uses an extension of the CoNLL-U format, a format which is used in the universal

Proceedings of the Joint 6th Workshop on NLP for Computer Assisted Language Learning and 2nd Workshop on NLP for Research on Language Acquisition at NoDaLiDa 2017

Level	Age	Training			Test		
		Essays (Sw)	Essays (SwSL)	Tokens	Essays (Sw)	Essays (SwSL)	Tokens
C-3	9	50	50	13,624	36	19	4,831
C-5	11	–	–	–	29	12	6,962
C-6	12	50	49	37,718	17	7	8,554
C-9	15	49	52	54,970	30	10	17,143
US-1	16	0	50	25,087	15	4	7,719
US-3	18	–	–	–	12	4	13,493
Total		149	201	131,399	139	56	58,702

Table 1: Distribution of texts by year and Sw/SwSL.

dependency project to represent part-of-speech, morphological information and dependency relations across languages (Nivre et al., 2016). The CoNLL-U format shows one token per line, with sentences separated by a blank line. For each token, it contains text and word IDs, the token, its lemma, part-of-speech tags, and dependency label plus head. For USCW, the CoNLL-U format is extended to also handle misspellings, for which an extra column is inserted, containing the correct spelling of the original tokens.

3.2 Data Used for Error Annotation

In this work we provide an added layer of human annotation on top of UCSW. In this layer we correct errors due to spelling, split compounds, merged words, and simple grammatical errors.

For this layer we sampled texts from the full UCSW corpus. We divide the data into two parts, one larger part that we intend to use as training data for NLP tools and for analysis of errors, and a smaller part intended to be used as test data. For the training data we aimed for texts that could be expected to have many errors, in particular texts from younger students, and texts written for Swedish as a second language. The main purpose for this decision was that we wanted to have a high number of errors in the data set in order to be able to train models for error correction. For the test data we aimed at a wider and more representative selection containing student texts that have been used as benchmarks in the national tests, illustrating different levels of achievement. Table 1 describes the data in the training and test sets. C refers to compulsory school, which comprises primary and lower secondary school. US refers to upper secondary school, which is not compulsory but attended by a large majority of Swedish youths.

4 Annotation

In this section we describe the error categories that were used in the manual annotation, the annotation process, and the guidelines used. We also present inter-annotator agreement for the annotators and give a summary of the identified errors.

4.1 Error Categories

The main goal of this annotation project was to find errors due to spelling, split compounds, and merged words. When we started the work we realized that it was easy to annotate simple grammatical errors at the same time. As a starting point, we decided to identify grammatical errors that only affected single words. This mainly included morphological errors and extra words.

Spelling is together with compounds the most important error type in this project. It is an error where a word is spelled incorrectly. The annotation does not consider the difference between spelling errors due to typing errors/slip of the pen, and errors due to lack of spelling competence. We include both words that are misspelled into a non-word, like *kännislor/känslor* ('feelings'), and words that are misspelled in context, but happens to form another existing word, like *ända/enda* ('end/only'). To judge if a word is correctly spelled we use SAOL, Svenska Akademiens ordlista (2006; 2015). If a spelling is accepted by SAOL, we accept it as well. This include words with alternative spellings *idag/i dag* ('today) and words with accepted informal variants *sån/sådan* ('such') and *dej/dig* ('you' Accusative). We thus allow informal spelling versions of words, as long as they are included in the SAOL dictionary, and do not enforce a particular stylistic register on the spelling norms we use. Words that are misspellings of informal spelling variants are corrected to the informal version, i.e. *non* is changed to *nån*, not to the more formal *någon* ('someone'). For foreign words that are part of the Swedish text, for instance movie titles or sport terms, we correct any wrong spellings into the correct foreign spelling, if it is known to the annotators, and mark them as foreign words. An example is the English

Proceedings of the Joint 6th Workshop on NLP for Computer Assisted Language Learning and 2nd Workshop on NLP for Research on Language Acquisition at NoDaLiDa 2017

back flipp→back flip.

We also include as spelling errors cases where a word has the wrong casing, for instance for proper names: *carolina→Carolina*, or at the beginning of sentences, and errors with punctuation within words as in abbreviations: *tex→t.ex.* (*e.g.*) or hyphenated compounds: *sand-låda→sandlåda* ('sand box'). For the purpose of analysis we divide the spelling errors into two groups, **casing** errors, which only concern upper/lower case of letters, and all other spelling errors.

Split compounds are cases where words that should have been written as a closed compound has instead been written as two words: *jätte bra→jättebra* ('very good'). For words that belong to a compound but that are also misspelled or have the wrong form, we correct the spelling of each part as well. In this category we also include words that are not strictly compounds, but that needs to be merged to become correct words, like *för svar→försvar* ('defense') and *kämpa de→kämpade* ('struggled') or hyphenated cases like *schim- pans→schimpans* ('chimpanzee').

Merged words are in some sense an opposite to split compounds, involving cases where two words that are supposed to be written as individual words have instead been written as one word. Examples are *tillexempel→till exempel* ('for instance') and *iår→i år* ('this year').

Simple **grammatical** errors are in this work a grouping of some different errors that concerns individual words. We view this part of the annotation as work in progress, and do not have subcategories for these errors in the annotation; we only mark them as belonging to the group of simple grammatical errors. We restrict ourselves to one-word errors to start with. The most common type of grammatical errors are morphological errors, such as agreement errors *det är viktig→det är viktigt* ('it is important') and wrong form of words *en lite by→en liten by* ('a small village'). When two words have been confused, we annotate a switch of words: *bryr som om→bryr sig om* ('cares about'). Words that have been prolonged or otherwise marked for some kind of effect are changed into their canonical version: *såååååå→så* ('so'). While it can be debated if these cases are real errors, they are problematic for automatic tools like taggers and parsers, and thus we annotate them. Finally, we annotate extra

words in the text, by removing them. This could both be due to erroneous repetition: *det var igår han han klev→det var igår han klev* ('it was yesterday he stepped') or be wrong for grammatical reasons: *är en dålig på att simma→är dålig på att simma* ('is bad at swimming'). This category of errors is quite diverse, and we view this annotation as preliminary. We believe there will be the need of further sub-classification at a later stage of the annotation project, which we intend to base on already existing error annotation schemes.

There are cases where an error has more than one type. In Figure 1, the last word has both a spelling error and a morphological error, and the split compound has a misspelling of one of its components. While all types of errors are corrected in these cases, for brevity and clarity of the analysis in this paper, we will mainly count each error as one type, given preference to split compounds, merged words, and simple grammatical errors in that order.

4.2 Guidelines and Problematic Cases

To aid annotation, guidelines were put together, detailing the error categories described above, and how to annotate them. The guidelines also contained numerous examples of annotations, and discussion of some borderline cases. In this section we will give some examples of problematic cases and how we choose to annotate them, in order to give some insight into this process.

The borderline between a morphological error and a spelling error is not always completely clear. As an example we have verb forms like *hon to→hon tog* ('she took'), where the verb has a form *to*, which does not coincide with another verb form, but rather is the informal spoken pronunciation of the past verb form *tog*. For cases like this we use the strategy to annotate this as a spelling error if the student's spelling does not coincide with another verb form, and it is not clearly a misspelled erroneous verb form. A related case is the spelling of regular past verb forms, in the informal spoken form, which coincides with infinitive: *Jag svara→Jag svarade* ('I answered'). In this case, we annotate it as a simple grammatical error, since the verb form is wrong, not the spelling.

We are annotating cases where wrong words are used. However, it is often quite hard to tell which word is wrong, and what it should be exchanged

P-ID	S-ID	word	Auto-correct	Manual correct	Comment	Gloss
5.5	13	är	är	är		*is*
5.5	14	bläck	bläck	bläck		*ink*
5.5	15	fäj	väj	väj		*color*
5.5	16	.	.	.		
5.6	1	När	När	När		*When*
5.6	2	Bläckfisken	Bläckfisken	bläckfisken		*octopus*
5.6	3	Mar	Mar	Mar		*feels*
5.6	4	dolig	dålig	dålig		*bad*
5.5	13	är	är	är		*is*
5.5	14-15			bläckfärg		*ink color*
5.5	14	bläck				*ink*
5.5	15	fäj		färg		*color*
5.5	16	.	.	.		
5.6	1	När	När	När		*When*
5.6	2	Bläckfisken	Bläckfisken	bläckfisken		*octopus*
5.6	3	Mar	Mar	mår		*feels*
5.6	4	dolig	dålig	dåligt	x	*bad*

Figure 1: Sample of the format used for annotation: ... *är bläck fäj. När Bläckfisken Mar dolig* ... ('... is ink color. When the octopus feels bad ...'). Top: before annotation, bottom: after annotation.

with, if there are other errors or strange formulations nearby. In Example (1), it is quite clear that the preposition *av* is wrong, and that it should be exchanged to *genom*. In Example (2), however, the preposition *upp* seems wrong, but it is not clear what it should be changed to, rather the whole phrase needs to be rephrased. In such examples we do not annotate anything, since that is beyond the scope of the current project.

(1) så försvarar dom sig   av (genom) att
     so defends them themselves of (by)   to
     svälja vatten
     swallow water

     'so they defend themselves by swallowing water'

(2) När den sener (känner) sig hotad   så
     When it feels   itself threatened so
     sveljer (sväljer) upp (?) vatten
     swollows   up (?) water
     'When it feels threatened it swollows up [sic] water'

Another issue is morphological errors that require some kind of long-distance information to be resolved. We decided that these should be annotated as well, if they are clear from the context, even if far away. An example is shown in (3). However, when we change these types of errors it could lead to other errors, that were originally correct in the context, as shown in (4), where a correction of the co-referring pronoun from plural to singular, means that the adjective *skrämda* will have the incorrect form, whereas it was correct in the original text. In such cases we correct the adjective as well, but mark it as a grammatical error that is a consequence of the other corrections.

(3) När bläckfisken blir   rädd   så
     When octopus.DEF becomes scared so
     sprutar dom (den) bläck.
     sprays them (it) ink.
     'When the octopus becomes scared, it sprays ink.'

(4) Bläckfisken är blå och de   (den) blir
     Octopus.DEF is blue and they (it) become
     ofta skrämda   (skrämd)
     often scared.WEAK (scared.STRONG)
     'The octopus is blue and it often becomes scared'

4.3 Annotation process

The annotation was performed by four annotators, all native speakers of Swedish. Two of the annotators are computational linguists, one is a research assistant in Swedish and one is a student on the teacher training program, specializing in Swedish.

The annotation was performed in two stages. First we had a pilot stage with two phases, then we started the final annotation of the data, which is the version described in this paper. In the first pilot phase two of the annotators started work on the annotation, largely without guidelines. Specific issues were discussed between the annotators and the authors of the paper. At this stage specific guidelines were created, as described above. One of the original annotators left the project, and two new annotators were brought into the project.

Proceedings of the Joint 6th Workshop on NLP for Computer Assisted Language Learning and 2nd Workshop on NLP for Research on Language Acquisition at NoDaLiDa 2017

P-ID	S-ID	word	Auto-correct	Manual correct	Comment	Gloss
2.1	8	ihela	hela	hela		*in+whole*
2.1	9	kroppen	kroppen	kroppen		*body*
2.1	10	.	.	.		
2.1	8.1			i		*in*
2.1	8.2			hela		*whole*
2.1	8	ihela				*in+whole*
2.1	9	kroppen	kroppen	kroppen		*body*
2.1	10	.	.	.		

Figure 2: Sample of the format used for annotation: *. . . ihela kroppen.* ('. . . in the whole body.'). Top: before annotation, bottom: after annotation.

After a second small pilot phase, where the now three annotators discussed some issues and problematic examples, the main annotation work could start with finalized guidelines. At this stage the remaining original annotator re-annotated the texts from the pilot stage, according to the new guidelines, in addition to all annotators annotating new texts from scratch. Each text is annotated by one annotator, except for the essays used for investigating inter-annotator agreement.

The annotators are given texts in a tab-separated format with one word per line, and a newline to indicate a new sentence. For each word there is a paragraph, sentence, and word number, and then the word as written by the student, and automatically corrected by the SweGram tools (Megyesi et al., 2016). The automatic annotation is also copied to a new column, where the human annotators modify it to add their correct annotation. In addition we insert an empty column where comments can be added, mainly used for marking the simple grammatical error category with an *x*, to tell them apart from spelling errors. The automatic corrections were given as an aid for the annotators, but they were very noisy. An example of the annotation format is shown in Figure 1, the top part before annotation, the bottom part after annotation. As can be seen, all the automatic corrections are wrong in this excerpt. Spelling errors and grammatical errors are changed in the fifth column, and grammatical errors are also marked. Split compounds are treated by inserting a new line giving the line numbers of the sub parts, and the full compound. In case of misspellings within the compound, these are also added as corrections to the individual parts, as for *fäj→färg* ('color'). A similar procedure is used for merged words, where new lines are inserted for the sub words in the merged word. An example is shown in Figure 2. The annotators used either Microsoft Excel or a text editor to do the annotation work.

	All		−correct	
	Agree	Kappa	Agree	Kappa
A1/A2	.97	.96	.72	.65
A1/A3	.97	.96	.70	.62
A2/A3	.97	.97	.72	.66

Table 2: Inter-annotator agreement and kappa for the 6-way classification between error types or correct, including and excluding the cases where both annotators judged a word as correct.

Our annotation thus contains both the original text as written by the student, with potential spelling errors, split compounds etc, and the corrected version of that text, with respect to our error categories. After the human annotation, we performed automatic POS-tagging and dependency parsing of the two versions of the text, both with the original tokens, and with the corrected tokens.

4.4 Inter-Annotator Agreement

In this section we present results on inter-annotator agreement between the three annotators that took part in the final annotation process. In order to do this analysis, a sample of 2–3 texts each from level C-3, C-5, C-6, C-9 and US-1 were chosen, with a mix of Swedish and Swedish as a second language. In total there were 11 texts with 2923 tokens. The three annotators annotated this text independently with access to the guidelines.

First we calculated agreement and kappa (Carletta, 1996) for each pair of annotators in the final phase, for the 6-way classification of each word into one of the error categories, or correct. Table 2 shows the results of this analysis. Since the majority of words are correct, the scores are very high in all cases, but even if we exclude the cases where both annotators agreed on that a word is correct, the agreement scores are reasonably high, with a kappa value over 0.6, which is considered substantial agreement (Landis and Koch, 1977). In most cases the disagreement is between an error

	Co	Spe	Gr	Spl	Me	Ca
Correct (Co)	2,138		23			2
Spelling (Spe)	2	73	3			
Grammar (Gr)	15	4	65			
Split (Spl)	3			13		
Merged (Me)	1				7	
Casing (Ca)	17					23

Table 3: Confusion matrix for annotations by annotators A1 and A2, empty cells means no such confusions.

	Training	Test
Total	7,189	2,074
Spelling	2,826	1,205
Grammar	2,465	336
Split	548	218
Merged	192	73
Casing	1,158	242
Split+spelling	123	35
Split+grammar	29	1
Merged+spelling	46	24
Merged+grammar	9	2

Table 4: Different error types in the annotated data.

marked by one annotator vs no error marked by another. To exemplify this, Table 3 gives the confusion matrix for annotator 1 and 2. The picture is similar for the other pairs of annotators. We see that the biggest source of confusion is where one of the annotators have considered a word as a simple grammatical error, whereas the other annotator has considered it correct. We can also see that annotator 1 has identified errors related to casing to a much larger extent than annotator 2. For the other categories the number of confusions is relatively small. For the cases where both annotators have marked a word as being either a grammatical or spelling error, the agreement of the correction is over 93% in all cases.

Overall we find the agreement satisfactory, and believe that the guidelines together with the initial discussions among the annotators were sufficient for this project.

4.5 Error Statistics

Table 4 shows the number of each error type in the training and test data. The lower part of the table shows how many spelling and grammar errors there are for components of split compounds and merged words, e.g, the split compound *jete smart/jättesmart* ('very clever') contains a spelling error of the first component. When doing this analysis we realized that our current annotations do not identify cases where a word has both a spelling and grammatical error, as for the word *dolig/dåligt* ('bad') in Figure 1.

Overall we see that spelling errors are the most common errors in both data sets. Grammar errors are nearly as common in the training set, but far less common in the test set, which could be at least parly expected, since we have more texts from young children and Swedish as a second language in the training data than in the test data. Overall we find the number of errors in both data sets sufficient for doing further research.

5 Pilot Experiments

In this section we will describe two pilot experiments that shows the usefulness of the human error annotation layer of UCSW. In the first experiment we show how the training data can be used for training a simple spell checker targeting student texts. In the second experiment we show how much the errors in the corpus affects automatic NLP tools, exemplified by a tagger and parser.

5.1 Spelling Correction

We can take advantage of the human annotations of student texts, in order to train tools for solving challenges like spelling correction. In this section we describe experiments on spell checking using a relatively simple approach. First we investigate how our training data impacts performance of spell checking, then we compare the performance for different student groups.

One of the most widely explored algorithms for spelling correction is to measure the *edit distance* between an unknown word and words present in a dictionary. In our spelling correction experiments, we use a simple weighted Levenshtein edit distance approach aiming to correct misspellings in the input text. The Levenshtein distance gives an indication of the similarity between two strings, by computing the minimum number of characters that need to be inserted, deleted or substituted in order to transform one string into the other string (Levenshtein, 1966). Our approach is based on the method originally presented by Pettersson et al. (2013) for the similar task of spelling normalization of historical text, and is illustrated in Figure 3. By using a weighted Levenshtein distance, we can take advantage of the training data in the human annotation layer of UCSW.

Before any normalization attempts are carried out, the program checks the length and charac-

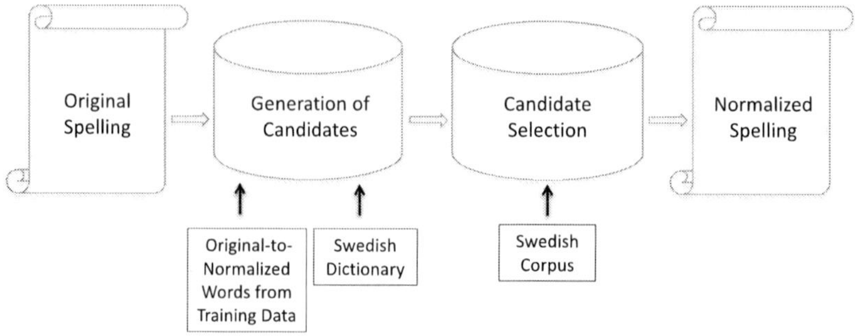

Figure 3: Flowchart for the spelling normalization procedure

teristics of the word. If the word contains only one letter, or contains digits, the word is left unchanged. Likewise, to avoid normalization of proper nouns, words with an initial uppercase letter are also left unchanged, unless they occur in sentence-initial position. One example from the test data is the string *Texten om Kissie, skriven av Malin Ekman i Expressen 10/6 2010* ('The text about Kissie, written by Malin Ekman in [the newspaper] Expressen 10/6 2010'). In this string, the proper nouns *Kissie, Malin, Ekman* and *Expressen* will be left unchanged due to their initial uppercase letters. However, the word form *Texten* ('The text') would be considered for normalization despite the uppercase first letter, since it is in sentence-initial position. The word form *i* ('in') will not be normalized due to its short length, and the date *10/6 2010* will not be normalized either, since it consists of digits.

For all word forms that do not meet these requirements, the first task is to find appropriate candidates for normalization. This is done by comparing each word form towards two lexical resources:

1. The training part of the UCSW corpus, with mappings of the students' original word forms to their manually corrected spellings.

2. The SALDO dictionary (version 2.0), a lexical resource developed for present-day written Swedish, containing approximately 1,1 million word forms (Borin et al., 2008).

If the word form is present in the SALDO dictionary, or if it occurs without having been changed in the manually normalized training part of the UCSW corpus, the word form is considered to have a correct spelling and is thus left unchanged

during normalization. Else, if the word form is present in the training corpus with a normalized spelling that is different from the original spelling, this previously normalized spelling is chosen as normalization candidate. For example, the word form *henes* is not present in the dictionary. It has, however, been normalized into *hennes* (correct spelling of the pronoun 'her') in the training data. Thus, *hennes* will be chosen as normalization candidate for the word form *henes*.

If the word form is found neither in the training corpus nor in the dictionary, edit distance calculations are performed, comparing the word form to all word forms present in the dictionary. If there are dictionary entries with a Levenshtein distance of maximally one from the original word form, these entries are chosen as normalization candidates. The reason for choosing one as the maximum edit distance allowed, is that previous corpus studies have shown that misspellings usually do not differ from the intended word form with more than one edit (Kukich, 1992).

To further adapt the spelling correction process to the task of normalizing student writings, weights lower than one are included for frequently observed edits in the training data. This method has previously proven successful for example by Brill and Moore (2000) for spelling correction, and by Pettersson et al. (2013) for spelling normalization of historical text. We adopt the same approach as Pettersson et al. (2013). Thus, we split the training corpus into 90% training and 10% tuning, where the training part of the corpus is used for extracting edits to consider, by automatically comparing the historical word forms to their modern spelling, using traditional Levenshtein edit distance comparisons. The edits extracted from the training corpus are then weighted based on their relative frequency in the tuning corpus.

One example from the corpus of student writings is the replacement of *o* by *å*, which is given the weight 0.87, meaning that it is more likely that the system will choose to replace *o* by the phonologically similar *å*, than to replace it by for example *p*. Weights for sequences of two characters on the source and/or target side are also included, mainly resulting in weights for transforming double consonants (such as *mm*) into a single occurrence of the same consonant (*m*), or the other way around.

Once the normalization candidates have been generated, a final normalization is to be chosen. This is done based on corpus statistics, in this case based on the Stockholm Umeå Corpus (SUC, version 2.0) of text representative of the Swedish language in the 1990s (Ejerhed and Källgren, 1997), containing approximately 1,2 million words. If several normalization candidates share the same minimum edit distance to the original word form, the word form with the highest frequency in the corpus is chosen. If several candidates are equally frequent in the corpus, or if none of the candidates occur in the corpus, the final normalization candidate is randomly chosen.

The above described method presupposes access to training data in the form of manually normalized student writings. If no such training data is available, spelling correction using Levenshtein calculations is still possible. In this case, the only lexical resource available during the generation of normalization candidates is a Swedish dictionary. Furthermore, traditional, unweighted Levenshtein calculations are then performed, where each edit has the cost of 1.

We present results both for the case where no training data is available (basic), and for the refined, weighted model (refined). We report results in terms of precision, recall and normalization accuracy, when running the Levenshtein-based spelling correction approach on the evaluation part of the UCSW corpus. In this evaluation setting, precision and recall are calculated for the *identification* of misspellings, that is the instances where the algorithm has correctly identified that some kind of normalization should be performed. Normalization accuracy on the other hand refers to the *correction* of misspellings, and is calculated as the percentage of correct normalizations for the

	Precision	Recall	Accuracy
basic	84.9	57.6	70.9
refined	80.9	63.5	78.2

Table 5: Spelling correction results.

true positives.

5.1.1 Results on All Data

Table 5 shows the results for the spell checking. The refined method, not surprisingly, yields a higher recall, meaning that there are fewer instances of misspellings that have been left unchanged. Furthermore, normalization accuracy also increases when weights are included in the process, meaning that a larger proportion of the misspellings get an adequate correction by the refined approach. However, precision drops to some extent for the refined method. A closer look at the false positives that are unique for the refined method as compared to the basic method shows that this is almost exclusively due to real word errors in the training data. For example, the training data contains the correction of the misspelling *knakade* into the correctly spelled *knackade* ('knocked'). This means that for the refined method, having access to mappings of misspellings to their corrected forms, whenever the word form *knakade* occurs, it will be automatically changed into *knackade*. The problem is that *knakade* could also be a perfectly correct Swedish word meaning 'creaked', which results in a potential *real word error*.

Analyzing the refined correction approach further, the results table shows that about 64% of the misspellings are identified and normalized by the system. Among the false negatives, real word errors such as *varan* ('the product') vs *varann* ('each other') and *sätt* ('manner') vs *sett* ('seen') are very common. To deal with these, one would need to include context- or grammar-aware spelling correction techniques. Another common reason for false negatives to appear is that the original word form has an edit distance larger than one to the intended word form, such as *balletdansöz* vs *balettdansös* ('ballet-dancer') and *piamas* vs *pyjamas* ('pyjamas'). One way to handle these would be to experiment on different thresholds for the maximum edit distance allowed, possibly normalizing the threshold by word length.

Regarding the false positives, that is, the correctly spelled word forms that have been normalized by the system even though they shouldn't have been, about a fourth of these (47 out of 181 in total) are proper nouns in sentence-initial position. Thus, more sophisticated named entity recognition would be very useful. There are also some inconsistencies in the manual normalization of the training and test corpora, which affects the number of false positives. For example, in the training part of the corpus, the word form *sej* (informal spelling of 'oneself') has been manually corrected into the more formal spelling *sig* of the same word form, which is in conflict with our guidelines. This means that system will always choose *sig* as normalization for the word form *sej*. However, in the evaluation part of the corpus, the informal spelling has been left unchanged in the manual normalization process. The same goes for the ampersand sign (&) and the abbreviated form *o*, which have been mapped to the word form *och* ('and') in the training part of the corpus, but have been kept unchanged in the evaluation part of the corpus. Another aspect leading to an increase in the number of false positives is the occurrence of English text within the otherwise Swedish text, which is not recognized by the system.

If these instances are ignored, about two thirds of the false positives remain as words incorrectly defined as misspellings by the system (120 instances out of 181), mainly due to a lack of coverage in the dictionary for example for compounds such as *snöhäst* ('snow horse') and *elefantben* ('elephant bones').

5.1.2 Results for Different Groups

The UCSW corpus contains texts written by different kinds of writers; younger and older students (from the age of 9 up to the age of 19), and writers studying Swedish or Swedish as a second language as school subjects. To be able to study further the kinds of errors made by the different types of writers, the training and evaluation corpora have been divided into four subcorpora:

1. Writers of all ages, studying Swedish as a school subject

2. Writers of all ages, studying Swedish as a second language

3. Younger students: from the age of 9 to the age of 12

4. Older students: from the age of 15 to the age of 19

	Prec	Recall	Acc
Swedish			
in-domain data	82.1	62.0	75.4
all data	77.9	64.2	80.7
Swedish as a second language			
in-domain data	86.2	61.9	72.0
all data	86.3	62.6	73.3
Younger students			
in-domain data	91.0	64.9	76.0
all data	87.4	65.2	76.9
Older students			
in-domain data	72.8	59.5	82.8
all data	70.0	60.2	84.6
All texts	80.9	63.5	78.2

Table 6: Spelling correction results for subparts of the evaluation corpus. Prec = Precision. Acc = Normalization Accuracy.

Table 6 shows the spelling normalization results for the different types of writers in the corpus, where experiments have been performed for training on the training corpus as a whole (referred to as 'all data' in the table) and for training on the specific subcorpus only, for example only second language training data for second language test texts (referred to as 'in-domain data' in the table).

As seen from the results, using only in-domain training data generally leads to a higher precision, due to a lower quantity of correctly spelled word forms being erroneously normalized (false positives). This is, however, at the cost of slightly lower recall and normalization accuracy, since the system then has access to less examples of correctly spelled word forms to choose from, both in the mapping of original word forms to correctly spelled word forms, and when generating normalization candidates.

It could also be noted that the system has both the highest precision and the highest recall for detecting errors in texts written by young children (age 9 to 12). Studying the misspellings in this group closer, one could see that the younger children often make errors that do not result in real word errors, and are thus recognized by the system as misspellings, such as:

- writing one consonant instead of the intended duplicated consonant, as in *fladdermös* instead of *fladdermöss* ('bat') and *överaskning* instead of *överraskning* ('surprise')

- writing duplicate consonants instead of the intended single one, as in *tännka* instead of *tänka* ('to think') and *hellikopter* instead of *helikopter* ('helicopter')

- confusing phonetically similar spellings, as in *betång* instead of *betong* ('concrete') and *scoter* instead of *skoter* ('scooter')

- writing words the way they think they sound, as in *skriskor* instead of *skridskor* ('skates') and *sovenirer* instead of *souvenirer* ('souvenirs')

The young students also tend to use frequently occurring, common words that are often found in the dictionary when spelled correctly, resulting in relatively few instances of false positives.

The older students on the other hand (age 15 to 19 typically use less frequent and more complex word forms, that are often not found in the dictionary, such as:

- compounds, such as *regeringskritik* ('criticism against the government') and *stillös* ('lacking style')

- words that have (rather) recently entered the language, such as *chattar* ('chat groups') and *surfplatta* ('tablet device')

- slang, such as *ocoolt* ('not cool')

- abbreviated word forms, such as *o* instead of *och* ('and') and *iaf* instead of *i alla fall* ('in any case')

Interestingly though, for the word forms that have correctly been identified as misspellings, the system is better at correcting (i.e., has a higher normalization accuracy for) the texts written by older students. One reason for this is that since the older students often write less frequent and longer words, there are typically only one word in the dictionary with an edit distance of one to the original word form. For texts written by younger students on the other hand, shorter words are often used, where there are several entries to choose from as normalization candidates in the dictionary. To improve accuracy for these cases, it could be helpful to add knowledge about phonetics to the normalization algorithm (Toutanova and Moore, 2002), so that the system becomes aware that it is more likely that for example *cyckeln* should be normalized into *cykeln* ('the bike'), rather than *nyckeln* ('the key'), even if the two candidates both are within one edit distance from the original word form. Another reason that the texts written by the younger students are harder to correct is that the

younger students, more often than the older students, make several mistakes for the same word form, for example when writing *jik* instead of *gick* ('walked'). Here, *j* should be replaced by *g* and *k* by *ck*. Since the generated weights for frequently observed edits are not as low as 0.5, misspellings requiring more than one edit to be corrected into the intended word form are out of the scope for the current setting.

The second language learners seem to make similar mistakes as the younger children, such as confusing phonetically similar spellings (such as *slengde* instead of *slängde* ('threw away')) and writing single consonants instead of duplicate ones or the other way around (such as *hottelet* instead of *hotellet* ('the hotel')). One difference is, however, that the second language learners in this corpus tend to make more mistakes related to inflection, such as writing *tågar* instead of *tåg* ('trains'), where the *-ar* ending is a more common pattern for plural inflection than the null inflection that is correct for this particular noun. This should have been annotated as a grammar error, however.

5.2 Quality of Tagging and Parsing

In this section we describe a small experiment where we compare the part-of-speech tags and dependencies automatically assigned to each word before and after the manual annotation. For this experiment we use the training corpus. We used the SweGram pipeline (Näsman et al., 2017), performing tagging using efselab (Östling, 2016) and dependency parsing using MaltParser (Nivre et al., 2006). The tag sets used are the universal dependency sets both for POS and dependencies (Nivre et al., 2016). The purpose is to investigate the influence of error correction on tagging and parsing quality. Note that we do not have a gold standard for tagging and parsing, we only note how the tags change between the two conditions, not if they are correct in either case. We suspect that the tags are more correct after human error annotation, however, and this is supported by a small manual inspection.

First we perform an analysis separately for each error type and correct words to see how many, and how many percent of the tokens in each category that are affected. For split compounds and merged words we compare the tag for the full word with the tag for the final word when split, which is the head word of a compound. While this is somewhat

Proceedings of the Joint 6th Workshop on NLP for Computer Assisted Language Learning and 2nd Workshop on NLP for Research on Language Acquisition at NoDaLiDa 2017

	POS	Labels	Heads
Correct	447 (.4)	2,989 (2)	9,551 (8)
Spelling	942 (34)	994 (36)	887 (32)
Grammar	434 (16)	726 (26)	749 (27)
Split	109 (20)	247 (45)	316 (58)
Merged	108 (57)	144 (75)	139 (73)
Casing	96 (9)	138 (12)	209 (19)

Table 7: Number (percent) of confused POS-tags dependency labels and dependency heads for different error types and correct words in the training data.

POS-tag		Dependency label	
VERB-NOUN	170	nsubj-dobj	130
ADV-NOUN	152	dobj-nsubj	108
PRON-DET	90	nmod-dobj	105
ADV-ADJ	90	dobj-nmod	91
AUX-VERB	88	nsubj-nmod	72
PROPN-NOUN	85	root-advcl	70
ADJ-NOUN	81	root-nsubj	66
VERB-ADJ	81	nsubj-det	61

Table 8: The most commonly confused POS-tags and dependency labels before and after error correction.

of a simplification, it can still give some idea of the influence on tagging and parsing. Table 7 shows the results. There are overall many confusions for both tools, indicating that errors indeed do cause problems for these tools. We can see that in all cases parsing is more influenced than tagging, always for predicting the correct label and mostly for predicting the head of each word. This can in part be caused by the size of the tag sets, since there are 17 universal POS-tags and 37 universal dependency labels. For spelling errors the difference between the number of tagging and parsing errors is quite small, whereas it is large for all other types. While the erroneous words are affected more than the correct words, also correct words are affected by error correction, especially for parsing. Split compounds and merged words have a very high number of confusions, which can partly be explained by our simplifying assumption of heads, but it also seems that these error types are difficult to handle for automatic tools.

Table 8 shows the most common confusions, across all error types and correct words, for POS-tags and dependency labels. The most common cases are confusions between nouns and verbs, and between subjects and objects. These are distinctions that are vital for a correct interpretation of a sentence, which again stresses the importance of good tools for error correction. There are also a high number of dependency errors involving the root of the sentence, which is also problematic. All in all the error types are quite mixed, and there is also a long tail of less common confusions.

6 Discussion and Future Work

We think the described error annotation layer is useful, but there are also some remaining issues. The spelling, split compound and merged word annotation seems to be quite sufficient, except for consistency issues with the annotation of casing.

The grammatical error classification, on the other hand, would need a further sub-classification to be largely useful. In future work we also wish to handle more complicated types of grammatical errors, such as word order errors and missing words. In order to handle these errors we also need to update the format used in the corpus. It would be desirable that these annotations are consistent with previous error annotations carried out for other languages to allow cross-lingual studies.

We aim to have a single annotation scheme that covers both Swedish as a school subject and Swedish as a second language. This facilitates future comparative studies and the creation of tools for error correction. However, it is possible, especially if the scheme is extended to more complex error types in the future, that we need to have specific error types for the two variants of Swedish, since L2 language can both be expected to have more deviations from the standard norm, and have more cases with different possible interpretations of an error. Additionally we do not consider either the cause of errors, or how serious the errors are in the current annotation scheme. These are also issues that would be interesting to investigate.

The analysis of the sources for issues with the spelling correction, and to some extent the inter-annotator agreement study, also pointed to some issues with the consistency of the annotation, even though the overall agreement between annotators is substantial. We thus believe that our guidelines should be extended to cover cases that were inconsistent, like the decision on the correction of casing problems. Other issues were due to annotators not following the guidelines. Yet another issue that we have noted is that we currently have no markup for combined spelling and grammar errors, which would be desirable. These issues need to be corrected in order for the annotation layer to have a high quality, which will mean we need to do more

Proceedings of the Joint 6th Workshop on NLP for Computer Assisted Language Learning and 2nd Workshop on NLP for Research on Language Acquisition at NoDaLiDa 2017

human annotation work.

This paper describes ongoing work, and we plan to annotate more texts in the future. Specifically we wish to have a more even distribution of texts also in the training data, which would allow us to do more comparative studies.

In this paper we described an experiment on spell checking. The approach was relatively simple, however, and we plan to use more sophisticated techniques in the future, and also to address real word spell checking. In addition we have already started work on improving the identification and correction of split compounds, and we also plan to address merged words in the future.

7 Conclusion

In this paper we have described an effort of human annotation of word-based writing errors in student texts. We described the annotation process and guidelines used in the annotation. We found that we could have a relatively high inter-annotator agreement using these guidelines. However, our analysis shows that there are still some inconsistencies in the corpora, that needs to be addressed in future work. We described a small experiment on spelling correction, to show the usefulness of the annotated corpus both for developing NLP tools like spell checkers, and for analyzing errors performed by different student groups. We also showed that errors have a large effect on POS-tagging and dependency parsing.

Acknowledgement

We would like to thank Malin Mark for proof reading and annotation work, Caroline Warnqvist for annotation work, and Jesper Näsman for Swe-Gram tool support. We also want to thank the two reviewers for their insightful comments. This work was supported by SWE-CLARIN, a Swedish consortium in Common Language Resources and Technology Infrastructure (CLARIN) financed by the Swedish Research Council 2014–2018, and SweLL financed by The Swedish Foundation of Humanities and Social Sciences 2017-2020 (IN16-0464:1).

References

Andrea Abel, Katrin Wisniewski, Lionel Nicolas, Adriane Boyd, Jirka Hana, and Detmar Meurers. 2014. A trilingual learner corpus illustrating European reference levels. *RiCOGNIZIONI. Rivista di lingue, letterature e cultura moderne*, 2(1):111–126.

Tua Abrahamsson and Pirko Bergman. 2014. *Tankarna springer före: att bedöma ett andraspråk i utveckling*. Liber, Stockholm, Sweden.

Monica Axelsson and Ulrika Magnusson. 2012. Forskning om flerspråkighet och kunskapsutveckling under skolåren. In *Flerspråkighet: en forskningsöversikt*. Vetenskapsrådet, Stockholm, Sweden.

Yevgeni Berzak, Jessica Kenney, Carolyn Spadine, Jing Xian Wang, Lucia Lam, Keiko Sophie Mori, Sebastian Garza, and Boris Katz. 2016. Universal dependencies for learner English. In *Proceedings of the 54th Annual Meeting of the ACL*, pages 737–746, Berlin, Germany.

Lars Borin, Markus Forsberg, and Lennart Lönngren. 2008. SALDO 1.0 (Svenskt associationslexikon version 2). Språkbanken, University of Gothenburg.

Eric Brill and Robert C. Moore. 2000. An improved error model for noisy channel spelling correction. In *Proceedings of the 38th Annual Meeting of the ACL*, pages 286–293, Hong Kong.

Johan Carlberger, Rickard Domeij, Viggo Kann, and Ola Knutsson. 2005. The development and performance of a grammar checker for Swedish: A language engineering perspective. In Ola Knutsson. 2005. *Developing and Evaluating Language Tools for Writers and Learners of Swedish*. Ph.D. thesis, Royal Institute of Technology (KTH), Stockholm, Sweden.

Jean Carletta. 1996. Assessing agreement on classification tasks: The kappa statistic. *Computational Linguistics*, 22(2):249–254.

Eva Ejerhed and Gunnel Källgren. 1997. Stockholm Umeå Corpus. Version 1.0. Produced by Department of Linguistics, Umeå University and Department of Linguistics, Stockholm University.

Björn Hammarberg. 2005. Introduktion till ASU–korpusen, en longitudinell muntlig och skriftlig textkorpus av vuxna inlärares svenska med en motsvarande del från infödda svenskar. Institutionen for lingvistik, Stockholms universitet, Sweden.

Jirka Hana, Alexandr Rosen, Svatava Škodová, and Barbora Štindlová. 2004. Error-tagged learner corpus of Czech. In *Proceedings of the Fourth Linguistic Annotation Workshop*, Uppsala, Sweden.

John A. Hawkins and Paula Buttery. 2010. Criterial features in learner corpora: Theory and illustrations. *English Profile Journal*, 1(01):1–23.

Karen Kukich. 1992. Techniques for automatically correcting words in text. *ACM Computing Surveys (CSUR)*, 24(4):377–439.

J. Richard Landis and Gary G. Koch. 1977. The measurement of observer agreement for categorical data. *Biometrics*, 33(1):159–174.

Vladimir Iosifovich Levenshtein. 1966. Binary codes capable of correcting deletions, insertions and reversals. *Soviet Physics Doklady*, 10(8):707–710.

Janne Lindberg and Gunnar Eriksson. 2004. Crosscheck-korpusen – en elektronisk svensk inlärarkorpus. In *Proceedings of the ASLA Conference 2004*.

Beáta Megyesi, Jesper Näsman, and Anne Palmér. 2016. The Uppsala Corpus of Student Writings - corpus creation, annotation, and analysis. In *Proceedings of the 8th International Conference on Language Resources and Evaluation (LREC'16)*, Portorož, Slovenia.

Diane Nicholls. 2003. The Cambridge Learner Corpus: Error coding and analysis for lexicography and ELT. In *Proceedings of the Corpus Linguistics 2003 conference*, pages 572–581, Lancaster, UK.

Joakim Nivre, Johan Hall, and Jens Nilsson. 2006. MaltParser: A data-driven parser-generator for dependency parsing. In *Proceedings of the 5th International Conference on Language Resources and Evaluation (LREC'06)*, pages 2216–2219, Genoa, Italy.

Joakim Nivre, Beáta Megyesi, Sofia Gustafson-Capková, Filip Salomonsson, and Bengt Dahlqvist. 2008. Cultivating a Swedish treebank. In *Resourceful Language Technology: Festschrift in Honor of Anna Sågvall Hein*, pages 111–120. Acta Universitatis Upsaliensis, Uppsala, Sweden.

Joakim Nivre, Marie-Catherine de Marneffe, Filip Ginter, Yoav Goldberg, Jan Hajič, Christopher D. Manning, Ryan McDonald, Slav Petrov, Sampo Pyysalo, Natalia Silveira, Reut Tsarfaty, and Daniel Zeman. 2016. Universal dependencies v1: A multilingual treebank collection. In *Proceedings of the 8th International Conference on Language Resources and Evaluation (LREC'16)*, Portorož, Slovenia.

Jesper Näsman, Beáta Megyesi, and Anne Palmér. 2017. Swegram – a web-based tool for automatic annotation and analysis of Swedish texts. In *Proceedings of the 21st Nordic Conference on Computational Linguistics (NODALIDA'17)*, Gothenburg, Sweden.

Lena Öhrman. 1998. Felaktigt särskrivna sammansättningar. Bachelor thesis, Stockholm University, Stockholm, Sweden.

Robert Östling. 2016. Shallow learning for sequence tagging. Presented at *The 6th Swedish Language Technology Conference (SLTC16)*, Umeå, Sweden.

Eva Pettersson, Beáta Megyesi, and Joakim Nivre. 2013. Normalisation of historical text using context-sensitive weighted Levenshtein distance and compound splitting. In *Proceedings of the 19th Nordic Conference on Computational Linguistics (NODALIDA'13)*, Oslo, Norway.

Anju Saxena and Lars Borin. 2002. Locating and reusing sundry NLP flotsam in an e-learning application. In *Proceedings of the Workshop on Customizing knowledge in NLP applications: strategies, issues, and evaluation (LREC12)*, Las Palmas, Canary Islands, Spain.

Svenska Akademiens ordlista. 2006. *13th edition*. Svenska Akademien, Stockholm, Sweden.

Svenska Akademiens ordlista. 2015. *14th edition*. Svenska Akademien, Stockholm, Sweden.

Kari Tenfjord, Paul Meurer, and Knut Hofland. 2004. The ask-corpus - a language learner corpus of Norwegian as a second language. In *Proceedings of the 4th International Conference on Language Resources and Evaluation (LREC'04)*, Lisbon, Portugal.

Kristina Toutanova and Robert Moore. 2002. Pronunciation modeling for improved spelling correction. In *Proceedings of the 40th Annual Meeting of the ACL*, pages 144–151, Philadelphia, Pennsylvania, USA.

Elena Volodina, Ildikó Pilán, Ingegerd Enström, Lorena Llozhi, Peter Lundkvist, Gunlög Sundberg, and Monica Sandell. 2016. SweLL on the rise: Swedish Learner Language corpus for European Reference Level studies. In *Proceedings of the 8th International Conference on Language Resources and Evaluation (LREC'16)*, Portorož, Slovenia.

Building and using language resources and infrastructure to develop e-learning programs for a minority language

Heli Uibo
University of Tartu
UiT The Arctic University of Norway
Landstormsvägen 12
68534 Torsby, Sweden
`heli1401@gmail.com`

Jack Rueter
University of Helsinki
Keinutie 11 M 72
FIN-00940 Helsinki
`rueter.jack@gmail.com`

Sulev Iva
University of Tartu
Ülikooli 18, 50090 Tartu, Estonia
Võro Institute
`sulev.iva@ut.ee`

Abstract

We will demonstrate Võro Oahpa (`http://oahpa.no/voro`), a set of language learning programs for Võro, a minority language in Estonia. When setting up and developing the system, we have made use of the infrastructure developed at the Saami language technology centre Giellatekno, UiT the Arctic University of Norway and the Võro language resources and tools – the online electronic dictionary synaq.org that also includes pronunciations; Võro speech synthesis; the morphological finite state transducer that is being developed as a part of the same project and a multilingual word list from North Saami Oahpa. Võro Oahpa consists of four language learning programs: Leksa – a vocabulary quiz, Numra – a program for practicing numerals and time expressions, Morfa-S – morphology drill and Morfa-C – morphology exercises formulated as question-answer pairs. The development is still in progress but the programs have already used within the Võro language course at the University of Tartu. We discuss the issues specific for Võro and show how combining the existing infrastructure, resources and experiences can make the development of a learning system for a language with limited resources easier and give extra values to the system.

1 Introduction

The Võro language is a South Estonian language with ca 70 000 speakers. (The Estonian written language is based on the dialects of Northern Estonia). Võro organisations (Võro Institute etc.) want to recognise Võro officially as a separate language which has been discussed twice in Estonian parliament Riigikogu, however, without positive decision. That is why Võro is officially considered a dialect of Estonian even up to now. Despite of this Estonian government supports the maintenance and development of Võro by financing Võro Institute – a state institute dealing with Võro language and culture. Võro also has its own official ISO language code 'vro'.

The Võro language is taught in ca 20 kindergartens (in so-called language nests) and about the same number of schools in South-Eastern Estonia. Altogether 450 primary and secondary school students are learning Võro language and culture or participating in other classes where the language of instruction is Võro (Opetajate leht, 2017). The kindergartens and schools are located in the area where children's parents or grandparents also might speak Võro but it is not necessarily the case. On the other hand, thousands of Võro speakers or people interested in learning Võro language live in other parts of Estonia and Võro Institute has got queries about distant courses of Võro for adults. Since 1996 the Võro language as a subject can be studied at the University of Tartu. The Võro language course is given every term and has a form of a traditional language course with auditorial lessons.

We are aware of only one other online program for Võro language learning that existed before Oahpa – the game "Mein Zimmer" (`http://edlv.planet.ee/meinZimmer/`) that has among others been adapted to the Võro language. It is a nice "find-a-key" game but it is focused on one particular topic and thus very limited.

When learning a Uralic language the most difficult thing is morphology. Although there are a lot of language learning programs available, most of them deal with vocabulary learning.

Thus, there was and is a need for free online language learning tools for Võro that would cover

Heli Uibo, Jack Rueter and Sulev Iva 2017. Building and using language resources and infrastructure to develop e-learning programs for a minority language. *Proceedings of the Joint 6th Workshop on NLP for Computer Assisted Language Learning and 2nd Workshop on NLP for Research on Language Acquisition at NoDaLiDa 2017*. Linköping Electronic Conference Proceedings 134: 61–67.

the basic vocabulary for a learner and, most importantly, the basic grammar. In 2013, as a part of a cooperation project between the language technology researchers at the University of Tartu and the Saami language technology centre Giellatekno at UiT the Arctic University of Norway, we started to adapt Oahpa, a set of language learning programs, initially created for North Saami and by now implemented for more than 20 languages, to the Võro language. The ICALL system Oahpa (Antonsen et al, 2009) is primarily meant as a supporting tool for learning vocabulary and grammar for adult students attending respective language courses. But as the usage statistic shows, a lot of people who do not attend any course, also use the system for learning North Saami because it is freely available on the internet. During a 6 months period there were 3,676 unique visitors of North and South Saami Oahpa pages (Antonsen et al., 2013) while the number of people who were taking the respective language courses was about ten times smaller.

So, Oahpa should be a good choice for the intended users of our language learning programs – the participants of the Võro language course at University of Tartu and all other Võro language learners whereever in the world, with possibly no or little contact with the spoken Võro and no access to Võro language courses. When designing the content of Võro Oahpa we are trying to meet the needs of both user groups. Our programs can mostly be used to support the students' individual training of vocabulary and grammar of the Võro language.

Other grammar learning programs we are aware of are e.g. Killerfiller (Bick, 2005) and ESPRIT (Koller, 2005). These are text-based ICALL systems where sentences are extracted from a corpus. In the system VIEW (Meurers et al, 2010), any webpage that is in the right language can turned into a grammar exercise. This is a fantastic system but concerning the Võro language, however, the material on the web is still quite small.

2 Existing resources and infrastructure

Thanks to the cooperation project we could make use of the Giellatekno and Divvun infrastructure (Moshagen et al, 2014) – a development infrastructure created to make it easier for people working on languages with limited textual resources to build language technology applications. The general idea is that (computational) linguists compose formalised grammar descriptions and lexicons, and the intrastructure makes it possible to use the lexicons and grammar as the basis for NLP tools (e.g. morphological and syntactic analyser) and end user tools such as proofing tools and electronic dictionaries. We got easily used to Giellatekno infrastructure that has standard places for language data (word lists, source code for the morphological transducer, Oahpa source files, documentation files, etc.) and standard procedures for the production of language technology tools and end-user programs out of these. The infrastructure is well suited for morphologically rich languages.

As one of our goals was to provide pronunciations for the people who live in the environment where they do not hear spoken Võro we decided to make use of the existing audio and text-to-speech resources.

One important Võro language resource is the online dictionary `http://synaq.org` that includes 15 000 entries in the direction Võro-Estonian and 20 000 entries in the direction Estonian-Võro. The dictionary also includes high quality audio files for Võro words. The audio files have been produced in cooperation of the Võro Institute with the Center of South Estonian Language and Culture and Laboratory of Phonetics, University of Tartu.

During the development of Võro Oahpa a prototype of Võro speech synthesis was developed at the Institute of Estonian Language. There are two voices to choose between: a middle aged man and a 11-years-old girl. The quality of the synthesized speech is good, very close to natural speech. The demo of the speech synthesis is available at the following URL: `www.eki.ee/~indrek/voru/index.php` and the software can be downloaded from here: `github.com/ikiissel/synthts_vr`.

3 Our work: Võro Oahpa – a set of language learning programs

We have a previous experience of setting up Oahpa for a number of languages. Although the overall procedure of setting up a new instance of Oahpa is similar, each language has some specific issues that need to be dealt with. For the Võro language these issues were:

- extensive spell-relax

- many parallel forms

Proceedings of the Joint 6th Workshop on NLP for Computer Assisted Language Learning and 2nd Workshop on NLP for Research on Language Acquisition at NoDaLiDa 2017

Spell-relax means that the program accepts different variants of typing for some characters. Checking of the correct answers must not be too strict because the written language is quite new (from 1990s) and there is no consensus on how to mark e.g. glottal stop and palatalisation; some letters of the Võro alphabet are missing from the keyboard layouts (there is no special Võro keyboard layout yet).

The illative and inessive plural of some nouns may attest to as many as 6-9 forms, e.g. the word *pereh* "family":
pereh+N+Pl+Ill: [*perrihe, perriihe, perride, perriide, perehtehe, perehtede*]
pereh+N+Pl+Ine: [*perrin, perriin, perrih, perriih, perrihn, perriihn, perehten, perehteh, perehtehn*], whereas the second person singular can attest to 3 if not 6 forms, e.g. the word *ehitelemä* "to decorate" *ehitelemä+V+Act+Ind+Prt+Sg2*: [*ehitelit, ehiteliq, ehitelideq, ehitellit, ehitelliq, ehitellideq*]

In the Oahpa exercises we need to decide which forms to accept as possible forms and which ones to display as correct answers. Whereas the parallel forms issue has to do with the morphology exercises Morfa-S and Morfa-C the relaxed spelling applies to all four games implemented in Võro Oahpa.

3.1 Multi-purpose side product – morphological finite state transducer of Võro

A finite state transducer (FST) incorporates both a morphological analyser and a generator. It defines correspondences between tag strings and word forms of a language. There exists a powerful FST development environment in the Divvun ad Giellatekno infrastructure. Using the standard file and tag names and other conventions makes it possible for a FST developer (linguist) to use the automatic build process that is taken care of by a number of filters and scripts. The compiled transducers can be used in several applications as language learning programs, online dictionaries, spelling checkers and machine translation tools. The Võro morphological transducer has so far been used in Oahpa and in the morphology-aware dictionary `http://sonad.uit.no`.

While building the morphological FST we have made use of the experience of developing morphology descriptions for other Uralic languages as the Saami languages, Erzya, Hill Mari a.o.

The problems we tackled when modeling Võro morphology were the following:

- Vowel harmony is not always predictable from the nominative or genitive singular forms, variation between singular and plural stem harmony, e.g. ("host") *esäk – esäku* genitive singular but *esäkidegaq* comitative plural.

- Consonant gradation [2] – as many as 4 grades: *häbü, häu, häpü* and *häppü* ("shame" nominative, genitive, partitive, illative singular).

- Many inflection types. Even if it seems that the word belongs to the same type there might be some forms in the paradigm that are different. The classification of nouns and adjective stem types has uncovered further irregularities, that might be dealt with through geographic/dialect classification.

- Parallel forms. For pedagogical purposes, it should be desirable that the preferred parallel forms are tagged differently from the non-preferred ones. Therefore, we have tagged all the non-preferred parallel forms with the tag *+Use/NG*. The non-preferred forms are accepted when the user enters those but not shown as correct answers.

We have applied the systematic error correction procedure of the FST:

1. All the simple words, i.e. derived and compound words excluded, have been generated by the FST as a large table.

2. A testing person has marked the errors in the table.

3. The errors have been corrected in the FST.

New subtypes of the inflection types for both nouns and verbs have been described in the FST as a result of this systematic work. For example, the noun types where singular nominative ends with a consonant but the stem vowel appears in genitive and other cases have been split by stem vowel to 3-4 separate types. That was implemented by introducing new continuation lexica.

---

[2]Consonant gradation is a type of consonant mutation where during the inflection either the length of a consonant is changing, a consonant is replaced by another consonant or a consonant is disappearing. E.g. *supi : suppi* ("soup" genitive singular vs partitive singular), *anda : anna* ("to give" infinitive vs connegative)

Proceedings of the Joint 6th Workshop on NLP for Computer Assisted Language Learning and 2nd Workshop on NLP for Research on Language Acquisition at NoDaLiDa 2017

Currently all the 13260 yaml tests pass, i.e. the morphological FST generates correctly all the forms that are given in the tests.

The FST has also been tested on the running text (Võro wikipedia and children's book "Suur must koer"). The current testing results are presented in the table Table 1.

	Total	Missing	Missing %
All tokens	82 390	294 335	28%
Unique tokens	30 695	50 142	61%

Table 1: Evaluation results of the Võro FST.

For Oahpa the lexical coverage is good enough, as long as all the words that are in the Oahpa lexicon are in the FST. The most important thing is, however, that all the generated forms are correct. But in the longer perspective, of course, we aim at much better lexical coverage that would facilitate morphological analysis and spelling check of running Võro texts.

3.2 Online language learning tools (Oahpa games)

3.2.1 Numra – program for training numerals and date and time expressions

Numra is probably the simplest game that a beginner might start with. The easiest setup of the Cardinals game presents numerals 1-10 as the sets of five and the user's task is to guess which number corresponds to which word.

Three special finite state transducers were created to enable these exercises – a transducer of cardinal and ordinal numerals, a transducer of time expressions and a transducer of date expressions. The transducers define correspondences between numerical and textual representations of numbers, time points and dates.

3.2.2 Leksa – a vocabulary training program

Leksa is a classical vocabulary test where the user has to translate isolated words or everyday expressions from Võro to a metalanguage or vice versa. The drop-down menus enable the selection of words by topic (semantic category, sometimes in a broader sense): human, animal, food/drink, time, body, clothes, school, nature, work/economy, etc.

There are several metalanguages – Estonian, Finnish, English, German, North Saami, Norwegian, Swedish. This makes it possible for people with different language backgrounds to learn Võro vocabulary. To make Võro Oahpa more accessible

we have also localised the whole user interface to Estonian, Finnish, English and Võro. The lexicon size of Leksa is ca 1300 words. The core of the lexicon comes from North Saami Oahpa (therefore we also have translations to North Saami and Norwegian for most of the words). But we have adapted the lexicon to our needs – removed some words that belong to Saami cultural space and added lists of frequently used Võro words with translations to some semantic classes (alltogether ca 300 words).

We have also added audio to Võro Leksa – a possibility to listen to the pronunciations of the Võro words. The pronunciations have been integrated from the sound database of the Võro-Estonian-Võro electronic dictionary *synaq.org*. The words have been read in by native speakers of Võro.

3.2.3 Morfa-S – a morphology drill program

Given the primary form (nominative singular for nouns and infinitive for verbs), the task is to build a specific inflected form. For nouns all the 14 cases in singular and plural can be practiced (except for essive that does not have separate singular/plural forms). For verbs there are exercises on indicative mood personal mode present and past tense first till third person in singular and plural, including negation forms. For adjectives we have exercises on positive and comparative grade. It is possible to practice their declination in all cases in singular and plural. Morfa-S exercises are based on isolated words.

3.2.4 Morfa-C – morphology exercises in the context

The Morfa-C game is based on question-answer templates and the word form database that also includes semantic information. Each exercise consists of a question and an answer where one word is replaced by a blank that the user has to fill with a word in the appropriate inflected form. The semantic tags are used to build semantically plausible sentences. Despite of that, the sentences sometimes come out funny or inappropriate. Is it okay to present a grammar exercise where the policeman steals (vro: *politsei varastas*) or a priest drinks vodka (vro: *keriguopõtaja juu viina*)? For more advanced students the humor can be on its place whereas it can be confusing for beginners (also unpedagogical for adolecents). Our solution was a very fine-grained semantic classification. For example, we have picked only the action verbs suitable for Morfa-C present and past tense verb inflection exercises and added ca 50 verbs to this list. At the moment we have 151 semantic categories defined but the number will probably increase as we add new Morfa-C question-answer templates. Some semantic categories that we are using are listed in Table 2, together with the number of words in each category.

Semantic category	Nr of words
ANIMAL	71
BODYPART	41
FOOD_DISH	38
FOOD_GROCERY	36
CLOTHES	36
PROFESSION	20
FAMILY	20
WEATHER	10
SCHOOL	6

Table 2: Examples of semantic categories used in Võro Oahpa.

Another example. The question-answer pairs that are about buying and eating things require distinction between the food that can be bought from the grocery shop and the food that can be eaten as a meal. Often the food and drink words belong to both categories but not always. We also needed a special category for the food words that are natural to use in plural (things that we normally eat a plenty of, not only one, e.g. peas, berries, nuts). The lists of words denoting foods and drinks have also been extended with more foods and drinks that are common in Estonia or specific to South-East Estonia.

There is also a specific exercise for practicing back negation. Back negation has got a special attention because it exist neither in Estonian nor in Finnish. In Estonian, Finnish (and also in Võro parallel to back negation) the front negation is used where the negation word precedes the verb (e.g. *ei olõq* = "not is"). In back negation, the negation appears as a suffix that is added to the verb (e.g. *olõ-õiq* = "is-not"). There are more examples of back negation on Figure 1.

Morfa-C game in Võro Oahpa has a new feature that does not exist in any of the other implementations of Oahpa. Namely, the computer will read aloud the sentences (questions) using Võro synthetic voice (of a 11-years-old girl) when the user clicks on the loudspeaker icon.

A problem we have discovered was repetition of the identical exercises. This is partly due to the small number of words in some semantic sets but can still be avoided by improving the algorithm. There are three types of repetitions that we would like to eliminate:

1. Identical exercises within an exercise set consisting of three or five question-answer pairs should be prohibited.

2. It would also be good to avoid repetitions in the subsequent exercise sets. That is, if the user presses the button "New set" then the task words she had in the previous set should not occur in the new set of exercises, or even better – the words that she answered correctly should not occur but the words where she made a mistake could be presented again. But this idea is difficult or impossible to implement until we have not implemented the authentication of users and binding the usage data to specific users.

3. Avoid presenting the negatively loaded words (e.g. *ossõndama* "to vomit", *varastama* "to steal", *pelgämä* "to be frightened", *ullitama* "to act the fool") too often. That presumes a modification of the exercise creation process: weights should be assigned to the words (low weights to the words that should appear rarely) and these weights should be taken into account in the word selection algorithm.

3.3 Discussion

The most important question is: Would Võro Oahpa meet the users' needs?

We assume that most of the users are speakers of Estonian or Finnish. Therefore we need to focus on features of the Võro language that are different from Estonian:

- vowel harmony

- partially different case endings

- using of illative (the case corresponding to the English preposition "into") vs allative (the case corresponding to "onto"), inessive ("in") vs adessive ("on"), elative ("out of") vs ablative ("off"), particularly in connection with place names (there are place names that are used with different cases in Estonian and Võro)

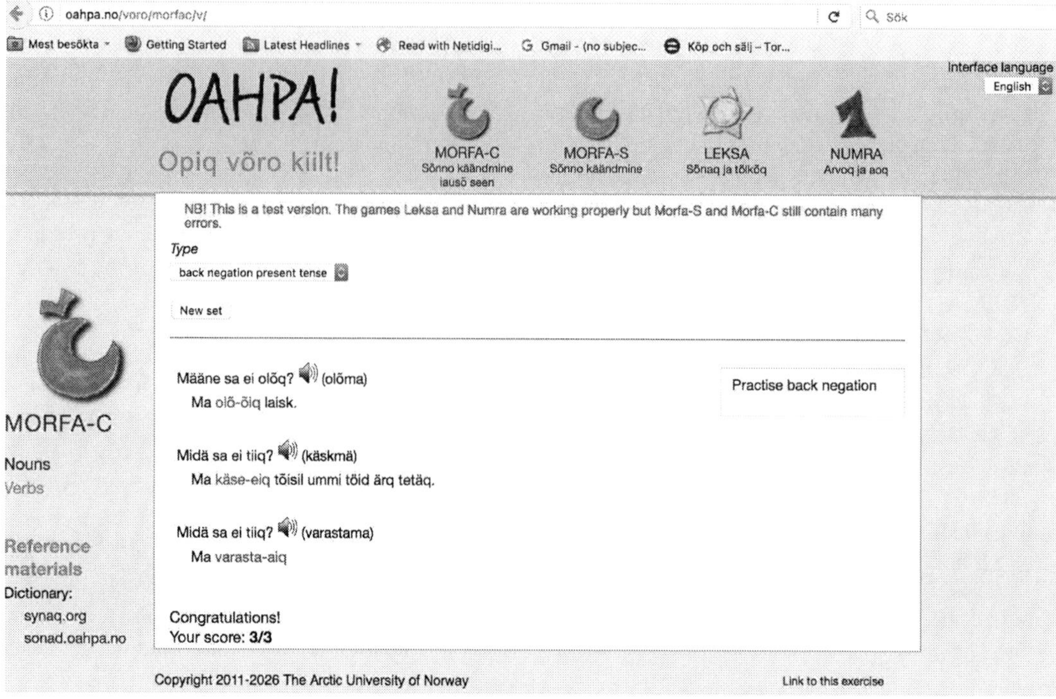

Figure 1: Screenshot of the Morfa-C verb back negation exercise

- two different ways of building negation: front negation (*ei olõq*) and back negation (*olõ-õiq*)

- different negation word in present vs past tense (*ei olõq* = "is not", *es olõq* = "was not")

- palatalisation mark in the written language

- more extensive use of diminutive

- pronounciation (especially important for the people who live outside of South-East Estonia)

All of the above, except for vowel harmony, also holds for Finnish speakers.

We also have to think about users with other mother tongues. Features that might be difficult for people with non-Uralic mother tongue:

- many morphological forms

- vowel harmony

- pronounciation

- usage of all the cases

All the listed topics are in fact included in Oahpa exercises in either implicit or explicit way but we need to create more specific exercises to make the learner pay attention to the particular features of Võro. For example, we have specific exercises in Morfa-C for practicing back negation and using the correct negation word (*ei* or *es*) but we should also create some special exercises on difficult inflection types, vowel harmony rules and diminutive building.

Võro Oahpa is free to use for everybody on the URL http://oahpa.no/voro. The authors will be grateful for any feedback about the system.

4   Conclusion

In this article we have presented our work on Võro language learning programs. This is the first freely available program for Võro that gives the users the possibility to train the basic 1300 words vocabulary, date and time expressions and morphology. While setting up and developing the programs we have made use of the Divvun and Giellatekno infrastructure as well as Võro language resources that were either created externally (online Võro-Estonian-Võro dictionary synaq.org where we got the pronuncations of the Võro words from and software for Võro speech synthesis) or within the same project (Võro morphological transducer). We can confirm that the infrastructure was helpful for our work. The biggest challenge is modeling the Võro morphology – covering all the inflection types, marking the preferred and non-preferred parallel forms and handling the different ways of spelling. Adding the audio dimension adds extra value to Võro Oahpa as many of the program's prospective users are not exposed to spoken Võro. Reading aloud the Morfa-C questions is the feature that is totally new – it has not been implemented in any of the previous instances of Oahpa. The work on Võro Oahpa is continuing to enable practicing of larger vocabulary and more of the grammar.

Acknowledgments

The work has been funded by The Research Council of Norway project EMP160 "Saami – Estonian language technology cooperation: similar languages, same technologies".

References

Lene Antonsen, Saara Huhmarniemi, and Trond Trosterud. 2009. *Interactive pedagogical programs based on constraint grammar*. Proceedings of the 17th Nordic Conference of Computational Linguistics. Nealt Proceedings Series 4.

Lene Antonsen, Ryan Johnson, Trond Trosterud, and Heli Uibo. 2013. *Generating modular grammar exercises with finite-state transducers*. Proceedings of the second workshop on NLP for computer-assisted language learning at NODALIDA 2013, May 22-24, Oslo, Norway. NEALT Proceedings Series 17: 27-38.

Eckhard Bick 2005. *Live use of Corpus data and Corpus annotation tools in CALL: Some new developments in VISL*. Nordic Language Technology, Årbog for Nordisk Sprogteknologisk Forskningsprogram 2000-2004: 171–185 Museum Tusculanums Forlag.

Thomas Koller 2005. *Development of web-based plurilingual learning software for French, Spanish and Italian*. Studies in Contrastive Linguistics. Proceedings of the 4th International Contrastive Linguistics Conference (ICLC4). University of Santiago de Compostela Press.

Detmar Meurers, Ramon Ziai, Luiz Amaral, Adriane Boyd, Aleksandar Dimitrov, Vanessa Metcalf, Niels Ott 2010. *Enhancing authentic web pages for language learners*. Proceedings of the NAACL HLT 2010 Fifth Workshop on Innovative Use of NLP for Building Educational Applications: 10–18

Sjur Moshagen, Jack Rueter, Tommi Pirinen, Trond Trosterud, and Francis M. Tyers. 2014. Open-Source Infrastructures for Collaborative Work on Under-Resourced Languages *Proceedings of CCURL (Collaboration and Computing for Under-Resourced Languages in the Linked Open Data Era) workshop 2014 organised with LREC2014:* 71–77 European Language Resources Association (ELRA).

Parijõgi M. 2017. Kool on kodukeele viimane kants. (School is the last stronghold of the home language) *Opetajate Leht*, 10.03.2017.

Association for Computational Linguistics
209 N. Eighth Street
Stroudsburg, Pennsylvania 18360

ISBN 978-1-5108-4337-0